Few people *need* encouragement as badly as the single mother who multi-tasks until she falls in fatigue and wakes to yet another day of the same—grinding along and seldom taking a moment for herself. *Everyday Single Mom* is positive reinforcement to those who have good reason to be negative and complain. It is a great reminder to the joys of the small things in life, is capable of lifting one's depressed countenance, gives hope, and reminds us of life's great possibilities. I recommend giving a copy to every single parent you know to offer daily encouragement for daily challenges. What a gift indeed!

—Gail Falzon, RN
CEO & Inventor, TMJ Pain Solutions

Shortly after Brian started writing this book, he consistently provided me with more and more chapters to read. I am a single mom and found his writing to be very inspiring. I couldn't wait to read the progress he'd provide. I truly hope everyone enjoys *Everyday Single Mom* as much as I have.

—Linda Atkins
Single mother of two

I highly recommend *Everyday Single Mom* to anyone. Brian Shell writes in a way that captures the soul and warms the heart. Never have I read a book where the author is so in tune with the human spirit. As a single mother of three daughters, the daily messages keep me strong and give me hope. Thank you Brian!

—Davida Anderson-Peak
Single mother of three

Everyday Single Mom is highly motivational. Inspiring and beautifully written, it lifts you up when you're down, encouraging you to live a more joyous life. Even the first day will bring a smile to your face. I thoroughly enjoyed Brian's exploration into a better philosophy for living your life. I highly recommend it to anyone and everyone who has ever had a bad day. It is sure to cheer you up.

—Teresa Kovalak
Author of *The Uninvited Guest*

This book can be enjoyed by all. It warms the heart and rekindles the soul.

—Lynette Jordan
Senior Coordinator—September Days Senior Center

EveryDay
Single Mom

God bless you!

Brian K. Shell

EveryDay
Single Mom

Life and Dating Inspirations

TATE PUBLISHING & *Enterprises*

Published by Tate Publishing & Enterprises, LLC
127 E. Trade Center Terrace | Mustang, Oklahoma 73064 USA
1.888.361.9473 | www.tatepublishing.com

Tate Publishing is committed to excellence in the publishing industry. The company reflects the philosophy established by the founders, based on Psalm 68:11,
"The Lord gave the word and great was the company of those who published it."

Published in the United States of America

ISBN: 978-1-61566-009-4
1. Self-Help / Motivational & Inspirational   2. Self-Help / Dating
09.09.03

Dedication

This book is dedicated to my mom, Carol Shell, who is perhaps the greatest single mother of them all! I love you, Mom! Thank you for believing in me all these years!

Acknowledgments

I'd like to acknowledge a few people who made this book possible. First, this book would never have begun without a woman named Suzanne, who contacted me via my Yahoo Personals profile and encouraged me to write a book for single moms. And also, I have to thank Yahoo's Personals dating site for the initial direction this book headed into.

Second, I give a tip of the (red) hat to Ms. Sue Ellen Cooper and the awesome ladies in my single mom's Red Hat Society for providing rah-rah support of this book. My mother is the "Queen Mum" of her chapter of The Red Hat Society, and I've learned to love all the gals she pals around with from all around the country. Ms. Sue Ellen Cooper is the founder of this fine social group for women over fifty, and this book wouldn't have been the same without all their encouragement and friendship. Kudos to you, Sue Ellen!

Third, I graciously thank all the people at Tate Publishing for giving me my first legitimate chance at getting my writing out to the world at large. Thank you!

Fourth, I'd like to thank Candy for her spiritual friendship during the last stage of this book's first draft as well as Theresa, who I call, "The *other* (single) mother Theresa."

Finally, there are three people who often kept me alive spiritually, financially, and lovingly during the dozen years of writing it took to have one of my many written works published. They are my mom, Father Thomas H. Cusick, and my best friend, Michael Merscher. Without all of you, I never would have reached this point. God bless you!

Introduction

You'll notice as you peruse the chapter titles for each day of the year that many of them were inspired by Yahoo's Personals dating site. There, a single mother contacted me and asked about what I'd written. When I told her about my previous creative endeavors, she suggested I write a book for women like her—a single mother. So I definitely have her to thank for inspiring the concept of what you're now reading. Without her, the initial idea of this book and each of the chapter titles wouldn't have been the same.

There will be inspirational messages about your children, your spiritual life, your love life, the beautiful nuances of Mother Nature, a few random poems I wrote, and essential ingredients to raising your kids, as well as just a healthy daily pep talk to help bring peace and calm within the abundance of each day.

Consider this book your chance to set all your worries aside and take a breath of fresh air. Allow it to nourish your heart, mind, and soul for the few minutes it takes to read daily. Feel its positive impact produce a wealth of deep thoughts or simply just a wide smile.

This is intended to be a book that is easy to take in on a day-to-day basis. Not too much to slow your day down and not too little to take the place of your day calendar's thoughts. Whether you're still raising your children without the father, or even if the kids are grown and out of the house, this book will have a little bit of wisdom for each single mom.

The message and content of each day was earned through listening intently to many single moms' concerns and cares, as well as living a vast life. Thus, I'd like to tip my hat to all you single mothers who have to face the task of raising your children without a father around to help in the everyday activities. You have my respect and admiration—each and every one of you!

One thing to remember is that the world doesn't end just because you've suffered a loss at home. If anything, look at it as the closing of one chapter of your life so that a brand new one can begin, with all the potential of an empty canvas with which you can create a masterpiece!

I encourage you to start reading this book on the page of the day of the year that you're currently living within and then just read one page. Then on the next day, read the next page, and so on. And don't worry if you miss a day or two; the pages are short enough that you can easily catch up on your reading with just a few extra minutes. If anything, it might be a blessing in disguise.

Everything always happens for a reason.

January

All Life's a Stage:

January 1

When we wake up this morning, New Year's Day, we all tend to have resolutions in mind for the year ahead. So much promise, so many days...

For an everyday single mother there is hope and joy, anguish and sorrow, faith and love.

As a single mom, you *know* love; it's in your eyes. It's in the offspring of your womb. Your heart is full; and yet, the love inside you often seeks a male counterpart. There are so many avenues to express this love inside of you; but it often requires wearing many masks, with many stages to stand upon and play the parts.

Each stage we step out on requires a different role: the romancer, the disciplinarian, the giver, the lover, the teacher, the spirit guide, the enforcer, the cleaner, the bedtime reader, the nourisher, the gourmet cook, the healer, and, of course, the mother.

So many roles for so many stages, each day different.

However, each role requires we *do* step onstage.

Life is full of stages. Each requires us to play a part.

So don't give up hope. Rise up. It's a new year!

Serendipity:

January 2

As we awaken with the early bird's call, it is often a subtle cosmic signal to start the new day with a smile that causes a domino effect of events to occur that will enable us to experience many minor miracles, terrific timings, and stunning serendipities.

A child's cry can often seem so frustrating, yet it holds the hidden potential of putting us on the proper time track, and it allows for a sudden synchronicity to present itself with a loving kindness that we can never forget and are proud to proclaim.

Sometimes that little bird's early call or child's cry at an odd time can yield a bountiful blessing, a fortuitous small fortune, or even a hidden harvest with grace and ease.

So don't stop the serendipity flowing through. Allow it to open your sail to a new world. And don't forget to dance through it all because the sudden smile from a minor miracle can help love to leap through and out from your heart and soul with delight.

Embrace it. More will come if you allow them to and acknowledge the arrival of each!

Seeking the Impossible:
January 3

The perfect relationship often appears impossible. However, a higher coupling is possible with God, and it was he who created men and women to unite as one.

So many times we seek a soul mate that fills all the perceived holes we feel we're lacking. And yet, that's exactly why man and woman were created equal but different. The perfect pairing completes each other. And in teaching a child that kind of caring love, your child will become greater than you could ever imagine. They stand strong and rise above.

So educate your young ones on the beauty of romance and the essence of real love to try and perfect their soul; for as they grow with the quality of a nurturing mother's love, they will give back to you as that special man gave his love to you to create them with you in the first place—the ultimate in human reciprocity.

The love that your children give back *will* make the impossible possible.

Playmate Wanted:

January 4

When you read this day's title, please don't think of the connotation from the men's magazine. No. Instead, think of someone you share everything with in work and play, laughter and sorrow, good times and bad. And when that man finds you and the everyday single mom that you've become, he has the potential to embrace all that you represent. And in that you will find acceptance, peace, and joy from a compassionate, masculine soul.

It's a feeling that we can't describe, but when it happens, we run to it and hold on.

And it fills us so much that we should never give up the search because heaven on earth is waiting for us to find it.

It's like a cooling rain on a hot day—precipitation that brings relief to body and soul.

Your love is in you and out there; never let it go. He seeks you too.

Genuine, Loyal, Compassionate Woman: January 5

A woman is one of the most beautiful beings God created. She possesses tender strength that balances and nourishes even the hardest man, but just think of her children!

For if she can melt the heart of a wild and difficult male, just think of the compassion she has for her child. And just as her child adores her for her love, that man will do the same.

A young one always needs genuine loyalty from Mom. And in return, if that child is raised with loving kindness, he or she blossoms into a full human being.

Part of that compassionate and genuine loyalty to her offspring is to see that they grow strong and healthy. A mother will always worry; however, her smiles when they reach their pinnacle will make all the struggles they faced to get there seem worth it.

Therefore, if you're a single mother, and your mom is still alive, be there for her in her old age. And if, unfortunately, she's passed away, never stop praying for her soul. She needs you at *every* stage.

Seeing What's Out There:

January 6

We stand in sapphire silence on the shoulders of giants. One of the strongest giant rocks we stand upon to see what's out there is our loving mother. She is our foundation.

She supports you in even the strongest storm. She provides stable footing for you to stand tall. And she'll still love you even if you fail, for success is often on the other side of failure.

When we look out over our surroundings to survey the landscape of love and life, a woman needs a man just as he needs her.

But a mom always needs her child more. Her blood that flows through them is thicker than the water that man and woman swim within. And yet, while they mate in these waters of love, their union of tender caring can create life. And that life turns a woman into a loving mom.

Life Without Passion Is Dull:

January 7

Waking up without hope, without a passion burning inside your soul and spirit, is a very frustrating thing, often depressing, as life *does* have its highs and lows.

If that's the case, look into your child's eyes. Being so young, children still tend to be filled with all the promise of rising and unlimited potential. A child's passion and play are often so contagious that they can turn frowns into wide smiles of glee.

The one thing about being a human being is the fact that people need people. We *need* to see one another face-to-face, in person, for refreshment. We fill one another up!

So if you're lacking passion, perhaps from lost love, try to search out another soul with whom you can share conversation and a smile. You'll feel better when you do.

Need Someone Faithful and Loving:

January 8

Faith, hope, and love ... with the greatest of these being love.

Each one is necessary, though, to face the day with your head held high.

A hollow feeling from remembering the zest of youth *can* be replaced. But how?

Creativity is one way. Spirituality is another. When a mother gives birth, it is a creative process of carrying a child to term for nine months. However, your job is not done then, for you still need to see that the child gets raised the right way—with healthy strength.

Therefore, show that child the creative spirit. Encourage his or her creativity. Just as you created your child through an act of love, teach him or her other avenues of creativity: writing, painting, drawing, poetry, collages, architecture, sculpture, crafts, etc.

If you need someone faithful and loving, your child may be the place to start.

Law of Attraction—Just Be Happy:
January 9

When you look into a lover's eyes, you see the sparkle in his soul as he looks at you. That attraction you feel and see ignites happiness inside you both.

So if he sees you smiling at him, it will produce a reciprocal feeling in him too. And in turn, both of you will feel happy. Why? The synergy of attraction is the answer.

When man and woman were created, they were made to complement each other. Happiness in each other's company is a blessed feeling.

If you feel that way about a special man, don't hide it. Let him know. Reassure him that you care tremendously. And in turn, that reassurance will cause him to be the rose that finally unfurls his love for you.

The upward spiral of love ... much better than going in circles, don't you think?

New Friends:

January 10

A man named James Boswell was once quoted as saying, "We cannot tell the precise moment when a friendship starts … it is like filling a vessel drop-by-drop, which makes it at last run over; so a series of kindnesses … makes the heart run over."

Likewise, trust is a gift we can give. And by giving that trust to others, they tend to want to give it back to you.

> Friends forever is a blessed thing.
> Matter don't matter; people do.
> Build all your friendships.
> Smile the infinite smile.
> Strive that extra mile.
> Grace in friendship …
> … the rewards?
> Priceless!

No One-Nighters:
January 11

As we all go out in search of love, lust can sometimes get the best of us. Infatuation often only lasts a single night, and when it does, it's an empty feeling later on. Such strong hopes and desires get dashed and snuffed.

However, if you postpone immediate gratification of the flesh for a friendship of the soul, that new relationship may turn into something more than just one night.

Deferred joys purchased through sacrifice are often the sweetest.

So strive to groom a relationship with the one you desire; love instead of lust.

Choose permanence instead of instant passion. The resulting return to you? Time-honored and honed relationships that fill your soul with faithfulness.

Read the Fine Print:

January 12

How often do we take the time to read every single little word set before us? And if we do, how often is that information of immediate use?

Sometimes information overload is the result of reading all the fine print. On the other hand, if that fine print requires your signature, it is often *crucial* to understand what we're signing on for because then all those little nuances in the fine print can truly matter.

Likewise, in the language of hope, savor all the small nuances of every note and gesture.

In the expression of belief, let your spirit fly high, gliding and soaring through the skies.

In the law of love, allow the fine print to impress your heart and soul.

Courting—Is It a Lost Art?

January 13

For the single mom, "finding yourself" after the kids are gone is a tough act, for once the children are raised and on their own, you may find yourself facing an uncertain void.

What to do, what to do, what to do?

That's where getting back to the basics is essential. In a sense, we have to revert back to a state of youth in order to remember what we like to do and what fills us.

One step in this process of rediscovery is the art of courtship—long conversations without the TV on, leisurely strolls hand in hand, kisses without the thought of letting go, hugs that really make you feel held, flowers for each other, smiles that last, a firm handshake. Get back to the basics; the rest will arrive in time.

Sunsets Over the Water:

January 14

Seeing the sunset off of the reflection of another's eyes is perhaps one of the moments we will always cherish and look back on with a fond smile of remembering our youth. It's even more special when you see its sparkles on the waves of a body of water.

Sunset—much different from sunrise. Each basically looks the same; however, they each symbolize two vastly different things. One is a start to a new day; the other is an ending.

A kiss as the last speck of sun disappears can last a lifetime.

Moments spent in each other's arms as the sky's colors turn pink, purple, orange, and red can mean so much more when we are with someone who truly cares.

Each sunset contains a vast array of colors.

And as each snowflake is different, so is each kiss and hug.

Make the most of each one and try to do so in the glory of nature.

Drama-Free Zone:
January 15

Drama and freedom walk hand in hand.
Each has a stage it stands upon.
Yet they walk side by side.

A campfire in the forest …
A lone guitar serenades gracefully …
A songbird sings its sweet songs of many notes …

A gentle breeze makes the fire flicker and embers fly.
Each has a grace of its own; and yet, they walk together
throughout life.
The separation between the two is like night and day.

But when the grace of romantic inspiration strikes
us, it's as if the two were meant to be with each other
from the start—drama and freedom.

So don't be afraid if drama enters your life because
it may offer lessons to be learned for freedom to later
flourish.

Good Laughs, Good Times; Want to Talk?
January 16

Laughter, pleasant company, and good conversation are splendid things in life, and even the birds, geese, and crickets share it.

When tough times arrive, oh, how we long for those good times to reappear. And yet, life is a balance. It is a sinusoid of good and bad, smiles and grief.

But if you learn to dance through it all, you can achieve a state of balance.

And with balance, experience, and heartache, there is a wisdom that will arrive.

The past is the past. Let it go.

Move on and look to the future.
Make the most of today, for it is now.

Laugh, talk, love, and savor the good times.
They will come your way again. They always do.

Carpe Diem:
January 17

Seize the day, seize the moment, seize even the second!

Each day is comprised of many moments that fill your day. And in those moments, do you walk with a smile or a sullen frown? Is the glass half-empty or half-full? Will joy replace the sorrow that is in your heart?

A glass of ice water on a scorching summer day...
A cup of hot cocoa on an ice-cold morning...
A bottle of beer after a very long day.

Each has its time and place; and yet, each can make us feel so energized and relaxed...if only for a precious moment.

Therefore, make the most of this day and yell out, "Carpe Diem!"

Today's going to be a good day! Seize it!

Seeking Best Friend ... and Chemistry Too:
January 18

When you seek a best friend, you often find him or her in a form you aren't expecting.

They can be in the shape of a man, woman, dog, cat, child, bird ... or even God.

And still, when you do find that magically great being who makes you smile so wide, savor each second you share with them.

Each life is finite. Each second passes. However, if you make the most of whom you have and the chemistry they contain, you will always have memorable moments that will fill your memory with smiles, warmth, and joy, all of which are good.

Best friends for all eternity? Not such an impossible dream after all!

So dream "The Impossible Dream" always.

Who knows ... it just may come true!

Welcome to My World:

January 19

Isn't it a heartwarming feeling to see a doormat with the word *Welcome?*

It probably makes you feel that you aren't a stranger in town. And even if you really don't know your neighbor, a simple welcome with a hearty "hello" is always nice.

Words like *hello, greetings,* and *welcome* can mean so much to make you feel at home in a new place, in a new land. They let you know the host is glad you're there.

And even if that doormat is well worn and faded, that still lets you know that the host made many more feel at home here as well.

We all long for those who make us feel welcome. Cherish those who do so with a smile.

It's All About the Chemistry:

January 20

When you meet someone new with hopes of a relationship, that crucial spark of chemistry is either there or not. And accordingly, the direction in which that relationship will go can all be based on that initial spark.

Sometimes it's there; sometimes it isn't.

When it happens to arrive with gusto, grab hold of it and don't let go.

If it is strong, it will last. If the passion is there, the flame will ignite. And that flickering flame can turn into a friendly fire that keeps the soul warm on even the darkest days and coldest nights.

Chemistry is contagious, especially if it starts with the spark of love.

Inquire Within:

January 21

We all want to know what's inside another's heart and soul, for even in the darkness there can shine forth a brilliant ray of light.

And that light can shine so bright it radiates a warmth that pierces the shaded shadows. Even darkness is composed of a vast spectrum of electromagnetic light.

If the house is a rockin', don't bother knockin' ... just come on in.

If the doors are open with the lights on, walk in the entrance.

If they hear your call and say to enter, open up the door.

"Inquire within?" Accept the invitation.

Looking for Mr. Right:
January 22

There's a story about a wise and beautiful woman who was looking for the perfect man. She searched high and low for her ultimate male counterpart, bypassing many.

And lo and behold, one day she found him! Ah, he was perfect in every way and very handsome.

As she recalled this story to a close friend many decades later, her friend asked why she wasn't with him now. The beautiful, now old, woman smiled with a bittersweet tear in her eye and sighed as she explained, "Because as much as I was looking for the perfect man and found him, alas, he was searching for the perfect woman ... and it wasn't me."

What's the moral of the story?

Make the most out of the bountiful blessings that are abundant today.

No human being will ever be perfect in every way; always remember that.

Please Don't Make Me Sorry I Did This: January 23

Isn't it better to have loved and lost than to never have loved at all?

If you choose not to decide so as not to get hurt, you still have made a choice.

So many people are afraid to put themselves out there on the stage of life, and they live with regret later on because of it. Don't live your life that way. Never ask "What if?"

Instead, be willing to put yourself out there in the spotlight. Be willing to throw yourself fully into a relationship. Be willing, as a woman, to cross a crowded room to meet the man you desire and long for. Take the chance to succeed.

If anything, the confidence you show that man will endear you to him more. A little bit of proactive participation is worth the risk. Regret is the alternative.

Are You "the One"?

January 24

So many times I've met a woman I thought was "the one" I'd been waiting for.

So many times I've been disappointed, not by taking the initiative to make it happen, but because she wouldn't or couldn't meet me halfway.

If you don't understand what it means to reciprocate your love and feelings for a special man, that man may bypass you for someone who strides that extra mile in order to meet him halfway in all he does for her.

Life is about balance. A fifty-fifty mutual respect should exist.

Give too much, and you might feel used. Don't give back enough, and you might become abandoned.

If a man feels his woman is meeting him halfway in all he does, he *will* stay with her. If not, he may move on. The choice is yours. Balance. Respect. Reciprocity.

And yet, if you do all you can to please a man, and he still leaves, perhaps God is doing you a favor. Maybe that man wasn't one who could commit to you as you earnestly deserved anyway.

Somewhere Out There is My Guy:

January 25

A single mom sincerely wants to find the man she falls for and calls "my guy."

Every "single man" out there desperately wants a woman who completes him, his girl.

That feeling of togetherness is one of the splendid delights of being alive. In it is the fulfilling touch of another's love who truly cares to be by you. In it is the gentle embrace of two hearts beating together as one in syncopation. In it are two souls standing side by side atop a mountain of love, looking out in the same direction.

The fairy tale romance ... the tale of hope.

Believe that it can happen.

Be faithful that you will find it.

Love like there's no tomorrow just because you can.

A Water Drop's Dream:

January 26

I've seen the little water drop trickle down to find a larger lake; then the trickle becomes the stream, a stream searching the lake's deepest depths, a way to the river through the earth's cracks and seams.

A way to our purpose, a way to our destiny, in hope of finding, perhaps, a new way to achieve our dreams.

Yet a trickle must forge its own path, which is never safe and sure. With only gravity's guide weaving a way, belief becomes the cure!

It knows not the route to travel. In a path of steepest descent it goes. With constant changes going on inside, a small cocoon soon grows.

A butterfly waiting to be born. In God's grace it somehow knows... that someday its soul *will* fly free in the wind's currents, ebbs, and flows.

Life is never just the river, but it's a journey out to the sea. A human doing isn't a human being... until ya love whatcha do to be!

Come Enjoy the Day with Me:
January 27

A warmhearted companion whose company you truly enjoy is a blessed soul indeed. That being can be your child, a parent, a sibling, a pet, or even one you fall in love with.

The fact remains, though, that his or her company has a way of lifting your spirits to heights you can't achieve alone.

He may have a story to tell, or she may be the one who listens and laughs or consoles.

In any case, he or she should always be treated with the grace you would give a best friend. Because if that person is taking time out of their day to be by your side, you should value every second they're with you. If not, think about past times alone. Therefore, make the most out of the time you share together as friends, as lovers, as family, as kin, as one.

Artist Seeks Inspiration:

January 28

Every artist needs a muse to help inspire the next creation that sits in their soul, awaiting the moment the unique catalyst comes to precipitate its idea into reality.

That muse often comes in unexpected ways. At times, it's some nuance in a woman that strikes an artistic chord in the heart of a man. Sometimes it's something she says. Other times it's a gorgeous guy giving a set of songs to a woman for her to paint by.

Regardless, when that muse does arrive, treat them well, respect their wishes, spoil them.

For if they have given you an idea or an inspiration you didn't have without them, you owe them at least some small token of your appreciation, your gratitude, and your kindness.

Trust me.

Your muse deserves it.

Can I Buy You a Drink?

January 29

This day's title has to be one of the most basic pick-up lines at any bar. It simply means that that person finds you valuable enough to spend some money on you for your time.

If he takes a liking to you, you'll know it when he offers to buy another, asks to light your cigarette (if you smoke), or watches your belongings while you go to the bathroom.

And if he doesn't offer to buy you another drink, there may be many reasons for this, other than the idea that he doesn't like you. For one, he may have to be somewhere soon and only had time to share one drink. Or he may be waiting for payday to arrive and only had a little bit of extra money to splurge on someone other than himself. In any case, the fact still remains that he thought highly enough of your presence to want to spend money on you that he earned and/or received.

Thank him. You may see him again soon, and if so, who knows what may happen!

On the other hand, don't ever feel obligated to accept a drink from someone you don't care to communicate with. It's a woman's assertive privilege to just say "no."

Full of Life:
January 30

At the moment you're reading this, you are currently full of life. You are alive. But for some unfortunate souls in this world, this moment will be the moment of their death. If that type of moment does indeed arrive to rob you of the love of a pet, friend, family, or lover, don't despair. Of course, tears will come. But when the grief passes, and it will, you still have to face the task of life without that loved one.

If that's the case, take the time to grieve properly, as grief is never something you can avoid. No. Somehow, someway, you must go through it, and the sooner the better, while the memories are still fresh, while you can still do it right.

Let it pass over and through you. And it does take time. However, once it's gone, only you will remain, and you still have to go on living each new day.

Once it is gone, though, take the time to reinvigorate yourself by refocusing your attentions even more on those who remain that you love.

Your children are *especially* crucial right now; never forget them in this moment.

If anything, the brush with death you faced should make you appreciate them even more.

For Your Eyes Only:

January 31

When lovers share special and tender times together, they may pause a moment to turn down the lights and close the shades so no one else can see in.

We've all experienced times when privacy is needed and necessary for inhibitions to be set aside. It is those moments that make the memories last.

However, it is usually up to the host to make such a decision. They are the one who chooses whether what's to come is for you alone.

Or if you're the host, then the choice is yours as to how safe and secure you want your guest to feel in the intimacy of a tender time.

This is where electric lights go off and candles come on.

It is where soft, sensual music drowns out the sounds of the outside world.

It is where a soft whisper will last and echo, often with a love for the rest of your life.

February

Enjoying Life One Day at a Time: February 1

When you drift off to sleep, do you ever wonder where our minds go? It's a unique time of vision. Then when we finally awaken, a particularly vivid dream may linger in our conscious mind. It may even influence our upcoming actions during the day. If it was pleasant, don't be afraid to share it.

But even if it was a nightmare that lingers in our psyche, that doesn't mean we still can't make the most of the new day while we are now awake.

Each waking moment is a blessing. Each one is an opportunity to help another, to turn a grimace into a grin, and to do a good deed that randomly warms another's heart.

The clarity of waking lucidity produces a certain zest. Use that energy. Seize it. Enjoy your health. Count your blessings, and give praise for each and every one.

Never Too Late to Start Over:

February 2

When kids play a game, sometimes they do it so poorly the others permit a "do-over."

In golf, a particularly bad shot is forgiven and ignored by asking for a mulligan.

So if you find yourself grounded by errors, don't be afraid to start over. Then imagine yourself growing wings for your arms, which allow you to take off into the air.

If you imagine this, where would you go? If you were a bird, would you just stay by the bird feeder all day, or would you venture off and go to faraway places?

Sometimes we travel so much that staying in the safety of home seems like the perfect vacation. Sometimes we stay at home so much that we want to go anywhere but here.

However, if life sends you a signal to start over and begin again, ask yourself who you want to be and where you want to go in this next chapter of life. Then listen for your inner answer that means the most and respect those desires for the new start.

It's never too late to reinvent yourself.

Life is an Adventure:

February 3

If God knocked on your door in the middle of the night and gave you a calling, how would you respond to such a call for growth, adventure, and wisdom? And if you did respond, would you travel the world for him? Your life is never the same when he asks for a change. God is simply too strong. You *know* it when he calls too!

As the saying goes, "God doesn't call the equipped; he equips the called."

It may make you abandon an old life and pack up all your belongings; however, it is an invitation to come back home … and home is where the heart is.

Also, a house doesn't make a home.

If that's the case, even the detours may seem like destined paths, for even on an unexpected detour there may be a nugget of wisdom that awaits and makes the extra mile worth it. Who knows, you may even bump into a friend or even your soul mate.

Months spent by the ocean may be an opportunity to share a story of its grandeur with those who have never even seen the sea. God's calling is unique; share it.

All-American Girl:
February 4

America has always been considered "the land of opportunity." So if you're an all-American girl, you may possess chances to live "the dream" that others around the world only wish for. How do you respond to a land with so much promise and potential?

If you prepare your mind during the days of youth and encourage your kids to do the same, your older years and their journey into maturity may be more bountiful in the long run.

Yet some utilize their body rather than their mind in order to succeed. However, as you grow older, the body begins to break down. If you haven't taught your mind how to learn, you may face extreme struggles to survive.

In other words, teach yourself and your children the essence of working smarter rather than working harder. Isn't our ingenuity what truly makes America great?

America … it's the land of opportunity. Where is your future? Body or mind?

Trying Something New:
February 5

J.A. Stone once said, "No heart alone soars to the same heights that soul mates reach together." Therefore, if you decide to find your soul mate via an avenue foreign to you in the past, keep an open mind, for he may arrive unexpectedly.

An open mind to trying something new is the chance to don your explorer cap and chart unseen territory. Go out and find that new frontier... for you. Learn something new.

A new land often offers encounters that can send a soul mate in unimagined ways.

Each foreign land possesses natives who internally can now travel to new places in the stories you share with them, and in doing so, someone special may take notice.

Don't be afraid to try something new. You never know what abundant blessings await.

Your soul mate is probably praying for you to arrive at your destined destination too.

Everything Happens for a Reason:
February 6

So often I'm amazed at the cosmic coincidences that occur during a day. Traffic delays and tie-ups will put us in the proper place for a minor miracle to present itself with the person we had perhaps hoped to see. And lo and behold, that meeting will make us smile so wide and feel so good it seems as if it was "meant to be."

When these "chance encounters" happen, it's as if those people (I call them messengers) have a gravity that helps slingshot us into a direction we wouldn't have gone in without their "message," due to the time track we were on because of an earlier delay.

And the thing is that they may not know how the gravity of what they said or did altered our acceleration in life afterward, but in hindsight, you do. It's a destined intervention.

Each person has a gravity that can attract us into his or her orbit or even provide extra energy to propel us into a new life. When those messengers arrive, stay alert; they have an important message to deliver, which you have to listen for with complete attention.

The metaphor I'm making here is using "gravity-assisted spacecraft-flyby" physics to describe the natural leaps in logic that may help you recognize messengers easier.

Happy Being Me; Hope You Feel the Same: February 7

Many times when we hear about the fabulous lives of the rich and famous, we often wish we could be them. But is that wish one you would really and truly want? People in those circumstances are scrutinized by the public eye in every detail they do.

So count the blessings that surround you now. Anonymity offers freedom.

You may not live the most glorious or glamorous life; and yet, it is your own.

Each one of us contains a seed crystal that can be planted in fertile soul and that may enable a rich harvest to be reaped. And although that abundance may not be evident in earthly terms, our Creator may deem it very crucial ... and isn't that what really matters?

Find your happiness in your own life, flesh, and soul.
It is yours and yours alone to make the most of.
Lead it as God would hope for you to do.

Simple and Down to Earth:

February 8

Many people live complex lives. They're always on the go. And they become so busy that they don't have time for anything other than their commitments and obligations.

They may have a lot of work to do, which makes them wealthy, but is it *soul work?*

Sometimes we can get so caught up in the ties that bind. However, the light that burns twice as bright typically only lasts half as long—conservation of energy applies.

If you notice yourself falling into this trap, you may have to slow down to simplicity, taking a few steps back to make a few leaps forward, but don't burn out too fast.

Recharge. Replenish. Relax.

In the grand scheme of things, will you ever wish on your deathbed that you had worked harder in life? At that time, you'll be more worried about where your soul is headed.

Goo-Goo Girl Looking for Go-Getter Guy:

February 9

When a woman gets those goo-goo eyes for a go-getter kind of guy, everyone seems to notice. People seem to smile at the love that obviously flutters from her heart to his. And what a joy it is to behold when we witness that naked love in another!

She takes the extra time to look super special for him too. There is a slight skip in her step. Her heart is full. What a beauty she is to behold in that special time of her life. A spectrum of color abounds in all she says and does during a day. Her eyes sparkle.

When this woman happens to be you, don't hide it. Be like the proud peacock that shows your entire fan of feathers for all to see. For when you do, you give a gift to the world. And in turn, it will give back to you in the most unexpectedly pleasant ways.

A girl with goo-goo eyes makes us all break into a little wider grin, don't you think? Someday it could be you! So don't be afraid of showing off your strut ... because you *are* special!

Let's Explore the Outdoors Together: February 10

Mother Nature holds a special place in her heart for the single mom. She understands that too few recognize her diligence to make our earth a beautiful place, just as you try to provide a vast variety for your children in those days when their dad isn't around.

So if you find a new male friend who appreciates the outdoors as much as you do, cherish him dearly. He may make you see the outside world in ways you never imagined. He may offer insight into a variety of natural knowledge unknown until after you met him. He may make you take notice of the daily details you might have ignored before. When we see something through another's eyes, the bounty of blessings becomes perfectly obvious. You might even wonder why you never took the time to notice them.

> He helps your heart glide like a dragonfly.
> He enlivens an ordinarily dreary day.
> He makes you so glad to be alive

It's one of many reasons that you should never give up on finding love.

A Beautiful Smile:
February 11

The month of February is often a cold one for many people because winter is still in full swing; yet that's where your beautiful smile can warm the souls of many people.

So if snow is still on the ground, let your frown turn upside down.

The beauty of a pristine snowfall is only temporary, and spring *will* soon arrive. And as much as those cold days are hard to endure, there's something special about everything covered in white.

The white snow of winter offers a balance in our soul to the green leaves of summer, and that variety offers a robust change, which produces a beautiful smile.

Just think ... if you only had one season, instead of four, wouldn't you grow a little bored with the weather?

I'm a Keeper Looking for a Keeper: February 12

When a fisherman catches a fish, what makes him decide to keep his catch or toss it back? Perhaps it's a feeling in his heart that that fish still has some life left to live.

Likewise, what makes a woman decide which man to date? And she usually decides.

She is like a hunter in a deep forest, hoping to land that big buck. His antlers give him away. She knows in her heart who is the keeper. He'll cross a crowded room for her.

But what if a successful young man makes a soul change that makes him shy away from the money that once meant so much to him? Maybe he wants to find the meaning of life, or maybe he possesses a natural appeal to search for the absolute.

Would his wisdom, years later, be a treasure you're looking for if he was yours in youth?

If not, take some time to wonder whether money or wisdom will matter more in your old age. What type of man will be there for you in sickness *and* in health? What type of man will be there in good times *and* bad?

It's something to think about when you're looking for your lifelong mate.

Looking for a Guy to Have a Future With: February 13

The future is such an uncertain destination. It has many twists and turns.

You can try to have a plan for the future, but it always seems to hold something random you were never quite expecting when it does manifest itself into the present moment.

Having a future with someone special is a delight. However, changes often strike that none of us can avoid or prepare for; therefore, it pays to be flexible, to be spontaneous.

Depend on yourself above all others, but remain open to all who offer help in a crisis.

You never know when an angel will arrive to rescue you. In other words, if someone offers you a hug when you truly need it, don't question its motivations ... only accept the warmth that the hug truly provides.

An open heart and mind always allow love to flow a little easier.

Educated with Street Smarts:

February 14

This time of month is generally when Valentine's Day is in full force. It offers an obligatory nice night out on the town with the one you love. But what if a nice night is more special alone, with only your thoughts to keep you company? It *does* happen.

This is especially true if you think about the homeless. Often they *are* alone. Learning their street smarts provides an education unavailable in any school. You have to live through it to fully comprehend it, and if you do, pray that those days are just temporary.

Talk to any homeless person, and you *will* learn to see with a fresh perspective.

So in this Valentine's season, perhaps present one of those roses to someone who obviously needs a lift of spirits. Do you really need the whole dozen? Such a random act of kindness pays a dividend you never expect. Even the homeless need a little love.

Honest Woman Seeks Honest Man:
February 15

If you move into a new neighborhood, you may be a woman who hopes to receive a pie baked with love from one of your neighbors. And if that established neighbor does arrive with housewarming gifts of genuine concern, open your honesty to that newfound friend.

In these days of crime and deceit, there occasionally arises an honest person who shatters all misconceptions and shadows of doubt within an often weary world.

Some people question whether honesty is the best policy in a relationship too. And while speaking the truth about your feelings may set you free from a ho-hum union, then ask yourself if it was really in your best interests to stay with it any longer.

Couples can occasionally play mind games with each other to test how much their mates truly love them. Playing silly games to test the commitment of the one you really should love and cherish will only estrange you two in the end. Play them at the risk of your relationship. The mind game you play now may turn into the loneliness you feel later.

Truth tests are apparent when they arrive in a relationship. Honesty always allows you to pass them with flying colors in terms of your soul's destiny. Remember that.

Smile ... Life is Good:
February 16

A smile is such a nice gesture to give to others. Even if you're having a bad day, a smile can send that day into a better direction. It instantly can melt a hurt heart.

Just think of the first time your baby smiled in your arms after being born. Didn't that pristine happiness win a way to your heart forever and ever?

My single mom frequently recalls the first time I ever smiled at her that first day she first held me in her arms after my birth. There is a joy in her heart whenever she remembers that tender time. My first smile brought her an infinite wealth of warmth and elation.

Likewise, don't ever give up on producing a smile.
Strive to make another spirit's day with one.
Get a grin, say hello, and be yourself.

By doing so, the smile you give may produce numerous more from others in the future. And that in turn will produce a domino effect later on down the line.

Each one is special, especially if it is given with genuine respect.

I Am Who I Am:

February 17

How many people know who they really are? And if they do, do they give that knowledge out to others freely so they can learn to be your friend?

You are who you were born to be. No one else can take that away from you; therefore, nothing gets done unless you do it. Do so with cautious and classy elegance.

In my opinion, each person is provided with the same amount of talent and abundance. It's just what they do with it persistently from birth that matters. That's where a caring parent needs to take the time to create an environment that is conducive to success.

We all stand a chance to make a positive difference in this world, but how many actually put in the hard work necessary to manifest it into everyday reality?

When you're ready to realize your destiny, don't worry. It will come to you.

Take Me Out to the Ballgame:

February 18

The crack of a baseball bat, the catch of a football, the cheers of the crowd after a great play ... they all mean so much when watching in the stands with one you love.

That time together at a special event marks a magic moment in any friendship. Even saving the ticket stub for later memory recall can trigger tingles inside you years later.

If someone takes the time to invite you to a special sporting event, thank them in a wonderful way. Let them know you appreciate their thinking of you above all others when going to and coming back from the ballgame. They may soon take you to more!

A ballgame is a collection of a crowd to see a sporting event that means much more than the score, especially if those in attendance saw it with someone they truly cared about.

Film Femme Fatale:

February 19

It seems as though the golden age of cinema has passed since digital filming began. Now, we're never quite certain how much was captured in its natural glory.

For those of us who recall when a Friday-night film at the drive-in meant so much, we reminisce about our days of youth as "the good ol' days."

When I used to write screenplays instead of books, I did so with a vision of creating heartfelt rock operas that used music and nature in a unique way to tell a character-driven story. Now with digital filmmaking, a part of me is sad and feels that cinema isn't the same because it's so hard to tell what was captured naturally and what was created on a computer in the images we now see in theaters and on TV.

Do the digitally enhanced images really tell the same truth and drama as movies made in the past? I wonder sometimes … often with a tear in my eye.

It's kind of like the old TV commercial of an older Native American Indian overlooking a vast field strewn with tons of garbage. As he turns around to face the camera, you see a tear falling from his eye.

Are you old enough to remember that 1970s commercial? I now know how he felt.

The Beauty of Body Language:
February 20

The difference between a smile and a frown can say so much without ever saying a word.

To that extent, isn't amazing how much body language can reveal in terms of truth?

If someone isn't interested in you or in what you're saying, you usually instantly know by the way he or she avoids looking directly into your eyes in an important situation.

If a woman is attracted to a man, he can see it the way she'll flip her hair around, using it as a device to help him notice her inherent beauty without letting words get in the way.

Understanding the nuances of body language is an art form that takes time, experience, and attention to detail in order to learn its unspoken vocabulary.

The essence of attraction all starts with the way we hold our bodies at first sight.

Another's gestures reveal a lot more truth than the words that come out of his or her mouth.

Honesty is What it's All About:
February 21

Honesty is a double-edged sword. It cuts to the heart of the matter, and it can hurt to hear when we do wrong. However, you can learn from it more than anything else.

There's an old saying, "Never give a sword to a man who can't dance."

Likewise, how much honesty is enough and how much is too much? It's a dance to do.

If we were all brutally honest all the time, revealing every nook and cranny of how we truly feel, would we ever accomplish anything? Or would our feelings always be hurt?

We're all judges and juries as to what truth is most important at any given time.

Honesty and little white lies—which would you *really* rather hear? One reveals, while the other hides. One provides peace of mind; the other has you constantly remembering all the white lies you told so as to keep your phony-baloney story consistent over time.

Which do you prefer to tell?

Which would you rather receive?

Do unto others as you would want done unto you.

The difference often determines how well you can sleep at night.

Close Enough to Trip the Wire:

February 22

When we tiptoe through delicate situations, we must be careful not to fall.

With all the modern technology present today, we're in a wireless wired world. Therefore, it pays to be aware that almost everything we do now is tracked somehow. And even if all others don't know what you hide, God still knows and sees everything.

All that radiates can send a hidden signal, but the greatest signal of all is the sense of tingles we feel in our body when we inherently know or do something that is right.

Isn't that a pleasant feeling too? Divine goose bumps that send shivers down our spine?

If you're dancing a fine line when matters mean the most, a respectful dose of modest humility with a dollop of healthy caution can make the difference between success and failure, especially when that fine line can trip the wire that runs to our heart and soul.

Single Parent Preferred:
February 23

When a woman has kids to raise and is looking for a relationship, some will want a man who has children of his own too. Why? Because chances are he will understand her better than those who have never been through the style of life that her kids bring.

Perspective on raising a family can be exactly what a single mom needs in her male companion. Perspective on the cares and concerns of children can mean the difference between being inside a circle of influence or sitting on the sidelines looking in.

Regardless, each person you meet has his or her own problems to face. No one is exempt. Even the one who seems to have it "made in the shade" possesses problems too.

Problems plague us all.

We're all in it together.

Choose your mate wisely.

Life's a Garden; Dig It:

February 24

A piece of Zen wisdom you can ponder is this: "Not enough people weed their gardens." Taken metaphorically, this certainly seems to apply more to our inner state of being.

Is there an addiction you need to give up?

Is there a place you should stop going to?

Is there a person who is toxic to your health?

If so, pull that metaphorical weed up by the roots before it ruins your garden's grandeur.

Of course, it will take time to settle into the changes it makes. But if you can replace a bad habit with a good one, then change is good. The peace of mind will be worth it.

Dig deep in that garden all your life. The weeding you do may reveal a hidden treasure. Also, though, once the withdrawal symptoms disappear, you'll probably feel better as well.

A Passion for Romance:

February 25

When I initially created a personals profile on Yahoo's Personals dating site, this day's chapter title was the initial headline I chose to use.

The passion reveals my heartfelt desire to give my all in everything I say and do.

The romance represents what can make love leap in all our hearts.

Combine the two, and you possess the seeds for future relationships to grow, which may turn into being so unforgettable it eventually ends up in a marriage of love.

Those intangible qualities say a lot about a person.

To what degree do they permeate your being?

Try to nurture their presence in you daily.

Lost: One Glass Slipper: February 26

The story of Cinderella is one of redemption. In it a mistreated young lady finds a special man who appreciates her even though she endures so much disrespect at home.

It also is a fairy tale that holds a good lesson for each man, for when Cinderella accidentally loses her glass slipper in her haste to get home before her carriage turns into a pumpkin, she provides her prince with the "objective correlative" of her reality and true beauty.

For those who don't know what "objective correlative" means, it essentially is the one characteristic that represents everything about someone or some thing.

It is often a unique quirk that characterizes that creature with total recall.

We all have something that symbolizes ourselves. What is it in you?

Nice to Meet You:
February 27

Our first meetings are crucial.
They leave lasting impressions.
That's why we dress for success.

For a single mom, meeting a new man can make her heart beat a little faster. He may even make her feel like a princess, even better yet, like a queen. She might be the one a king lets into the kingdom he took years to create.

Are you a princess searching out her prince, or a queen in search of her king?

The difference between the two is maturity, wisdom, and savvy.

Not Your Average Goofball:
February 28

We can all be a little goofy at times.
We all have our idiosyncrasies.
We can be a little too silly.

But isn't that an essence of life that brings happiness?

Someone's goofiness can inspire us to shed some of our own inhibitions.

And while their idiosyncrasies may drive the rest of us a little crazy, chances are once they're gone, you won't ever forget them, and you may even miss them a little bit.

Every curse contains a hidden treasure. Lemons *can* be turned into lemonade.

It's all up to you to make the most of any seemingly hopeless situation.

Even a goofball can be a blessing during a dull and dreary day.

The Leaps and Bounds of Leap-Year: February 29

If this year happens to be "leap-year," what are you going to do with this extra winter day of the year?

If snow is on the ground, perhaps you should take this opportunity to go outside with your children and make snow-angels!

But whatever you do, make it an opportunity to do something you ordinarily wouldn't ... because leap year only comes around every four years.

Perhaps you can take your kids to a soup kitchen and serve the hungry. Another idea is to grab your snow sleds and go sledding down a steep hill. Even another possibility is to make a snowman in your yard—complete with a carrot nose!

Leap-year offers the option to make it one of the best days of your life. Thus, grab for the gusto and actively participate during this extra day rather than letting it pass you on by.

March

What You See is What You Get:
March 1

Is the tip of the iceberg all the ice there is? No. There's always a lot more below the surface of superficial appearance. It's like that with every person you meet too.

Some people only see the things we show on the surface and make superficial judgments. Yet if that person remains in your life, it's up to you to show the entire diamond inside your soul.

In all of us is a healthy dose of hidden wisdom that we can choose to share with others.

It pays to give everyone we meet the benefit of the doubt, up until they shatter our trust enough times that it makes no more sense to open our souls to them.

If someone owes you a lot, comes into a position of being able to pay you back, and then you never hear from him or her again, it may be the price to pay to remove that person from your life.

Butterflies:

March 2

When a butterfly flutters by, we may wonder what it felt like to be in the cocoon. Maybe it just doesn't remember, just as we don't recall being in the womb.

Life seems to hold numerous cocoons and emergences that allow us to fly free ... if only for a short while. In the case of the phoenix, its ashes allowed it to rise again. I imagine it to be like what happens to some of our souls when we die after a good life.

With that said, I'd like to share one fine day of memory with you. I was sitting outside, savoring a summer day in the shade. Then a beautiful butterfly fluttered in front of my face and landed on a nearby pine tree. Hoping to make its day as it made mine, I started cooing to it, telling it how beautiful it was and that I loved it. It seemed to like the sweet tone in my voice as I inched its way. I slowly came close and started petting the outside of its closed camouflaged wings. Upon doing this, it didn't fly away. Instead, to my amazement, that butterfly spread its wings and let me admire its full beauty, to which I ever so gently caressed them too. Finally, after a few moments, it decided to fly away.

It's a memory I hope makes you smile as I am now.

Caring, Sweet, and Generous:
March 3

March 3 marks a special birthday for a wonderful woman from my past; therefore, I can't help but honor and respect her memory every third of March.

She was an artist who encouraged me to title, sign, and date every creation I made.

Her inspiration years back still sticks with me today, and I now have many signed, dated, and titled creations in my portfolio that provide total recall of where I was at in life, due to her inspiration to diligently document every single one of my creations.

Likewise, I ask you to do the same with anything original out of your hands and heart.

As a single mother, you obviously did so with every birth of your children. And, obviously, you will always remember their names, birthdays, and signature styles.

Now, if your kids are grown and out of the house, perhaps today's inspiration will encourage you to create others things, such as art, that you can title, date, and sign.

You never know, you might become a famous artisan if you try, because the instant you became pregnant, not only did you become a mother, you turned into an artist as well. Perhaps instead of creating children as you did in your past, you possess a talent you should unearth so as continue a path to excellence that fills your days with creativity.

Down to Earth Yet Adventurous:
March 4

The reality of everyday has its roots in the earth we live in. Signs of the times may cause caution; and yet, adventure is often the medicine that cures days of ritual and routine.

Earthen roots are often what hold us, but adventure often beckons us to become more.

When you feel rooted and in a rut, a little variety may cure all ills, for variety is the spice of life. However, a plant with no roots only grows so much and soon withers.

A balance between the two is essential.

Does someone provide that sense of soulful balance for you?

If so, search that person out today and thank them.

They may happen to need you too.

Is My Match Really Out There?

March 5

Some single mothers find it hard to find an appropriate match. So many people seem either above you or below you.

However, there is still God.

He understands. He cares.

He is love to us as well.

When you pray to him for a match, what is it you're looking for? A friend? Support?

A human is merely finite, temporary, and mortal.

Sometimes we sorely need the infinite and the immortal.

Maybe it's why spirituality is such an important cornerstone for us all.

We each see God in different ways, but when we employ tolerance, peace prevails.

Tolerance and a compassionate heart are crucial for us all to get along.

If our home planet is destroyed because of differences, we all lose.

Young at Heart:
March 6

Youth is a wonderful thing. It contains so much potential. It holds all the possibilities of a positive outlook on what the future holds. When young, the horizon looks limitless.

When we lose our innocence and naïveté, it's a sad moment. It definitively signals that our youth has gone and passed into a mere memory.

But if you could be young again at the expense of your experience-earned intelligence, would you truly make the trade? I wouldn't. How do you feel about such a choice?

Is an opportunity to relive the past really a golden ticket?

It's usually tough enough the first time around.

The past is the past; let go and move on.

Love to Laugh:

March 7

Is laughter the best medicine?

If you're laughing *at* someone rather than *with* someone, then it is not.

A hearty laugh can release a great deal of stress, but if it is at the expense of another's feelings, then it actually hurts us all. When that person overhears it and lets the source parties know about it, then those responsible are the actual losers in the long run.

So don't cry. Even the best of us have been made fun of.

The "laughed at" share your sorrow with true understanding.

They were once like you and allowed it to pass with noble class and style.

Try your utmost to do the same.

Seriously Seeking ... Inquire Within:
March 8

Ask and ye shall receive. Is that always the case?

If we seek, what do we hope to find?

Also, is it really what we need?

A wish can come true in many ways, but is it always apparent?

Someone's trash may be another's treasure.

And it's like that with the people we meet too.

The stone rejected by the builders may become the cornerstone to the arch for others. It's all in how we perceive each other. A hidden solution soon reveals itself and remedies all ills.

So if you're seriously seeking someone, be open to all who arrive. You never know who may be the cornerstone in the arch of each and every day.

Do You Believe in Life After Love?
March 9

This day's title was inspired by a great song sung by Cher.

If you suffer the loss of a loved one, a void becomes obviously evident. Frantically, you search for someone to fill the empty feeling that resonates inside.

What do you do when feeling such emptiness?

It is life's way of reminding us that what we do doesn't always equate with who we are.

When you are always doing things, think of yourself as being at a digital state of one. And being that we can't be "on" at all times, what do you do to get back to zero?

Life after love or the loss of a loved one can be a cosmic signal for you to recharge your internal battery, to replace the negative feelings with new, positive friends.

Surround yourself with the ones who still care and then proceed to your next set of goals.

Success is on the Other Side of Failure:

March 10

Does a child inherently know how to play a Beethoven piano sonata without years of practice and many music lessons? It takes time to learn to read music proficiently.

Can you hit a hole in one if you've never swung a golf club before?

Did you drive a car without the correct key in the ignition?

Life is a series of mistakes meant to learn to manifest eventual success.

The essence of practice is a constant search for finding the right way to do things.

Success takes time, evolution, and many lessons to realize, but bliss does arrive.

As you strive to reach your next set of goals, persistence ultimately pays off.

Find it in yourself to never give up; success awaits your arrival!

Surprise Me:

March 11

Surprises can come in both good and bad ways. If we're not prepared for them, they can catch us unaware, and we don't know how to handle them.

On the other hand, if the surprise is in the form of a deed of random kindness that you bestow or weren't expecting, it can bring a warm treasure of joys, smiles, and tingles.

If you want those pleasant surprises to appear more often for you, perhaps you should do more random acts of kindness. When you put good karma into the world, it tends to come back to you when you most need it. If someone thinks of you, return the favor.

Often, the surprise we earn is the smile we receive from another when we do extraordinary deeds of goodness. Keep it going and watch the smiles roll in.

Rose Petals, Strawberries, and Champagne: March 12

Let's say you have a lover who is someone very special to the romantic woman inside of you. Let's also say that he has gone on a long trip. When he arrives in your loving arms that next time, try to take the time to make him notice you were glad to have him reappear.

One idea for you is to invite him over while your kids are away, have a note on the door for him to enter when he arrives, arrange rose petals for him to follow that lead up to your bathroom, and have a hot bubble bath awaiting him with chocolate-covered strawberries and an ice-cold bottle of champagne on a tray next to the bathtub.

Once he enters, turn the stereo on to some soft music, be dressed in some sensual clothing, and wash him with tender caressing care.

Trust me, it will be a night that memories are made of ... for the two of you!

The Cat's Meow:

March 13

Have you ever had a cat enter your life unexpectedly? If so, it may have taken some time to grow to love it tremendously. They *are* unique creatures.

When you pet a cat and rub it the right way, it responds with a purr to let you know how much it appreciates your love and care.

Cats coming into our life have a calm coolness inherent to the feline family.

Watch kittens play and see if their glee doesn't produce a wide smile.

Also, a kitty cat's curiosity can come in handy in alerting you to something it senses. They possess an inherent ability to detect dangers we do not. Their awareness of all that surrounds them is always amazing.

If you're a cat-loving woman, give their cool ways care, tenderness, and love. Earning their respect and trust is a beautiful thing.

Knows All, Tells Some:

March 14

There's a saying I use about people who think they know it all. It is, "Often wrong but never in doubt."

The one thing you learn when you learn is that there's still *so much* to learn.

Furthering your education often reveals how much there still is to know and understand.

When I was a graduate student contemplating my PhD, I asked one of my professors what his doctorate degree did for him. He replied, "It taught me that I can teach myself anything I set my mind on to learn, hone, and perfect." He taught me that a college degree isn't necessarily needed if you diligently continue your quest to learn about the things you love.

Thinking you know it all can be an empty experience because you have nowhere to go but down; therefore, open your mind and let it grasp the possibility of life-long learning.

Fling into Spring:
March 15

As the last gasps of winter arrive, this is often the time of year to feel optimistic about warmer weather arriving, and flowers beginning to bloom.

It's also a time when all the animals are mating for future families later in the spring season. Their loving excitement toward each other can be contagious too!

Therefore, try to teach your kids the joy of feeding those pregnant mothers of the animal kingdom so that their offspring grow healthy and strong. But remember, once you make the commitment to feed those hungry mouths, they start to depend on you to do so consistently. If anything, this is an opportunity to teach your children compassion.

Because the care you take to make sure those young animals grow can reward your family with newfound friends of all shapes and sizes. And in turn, your kids can grow into people who appreciate *all* of God's creatures with loving kindness.

Back on My Feet Again:
March 16

God can grant us nothing worse than giving us all we ever asked for at an early age.

On the other hand, he can help us get back on our feet again when we're down and out.

If your spiritual life is suffering, take some time to get back to the basics. Are you standing in sand or upon solid rock? We all need support; make it strong. We all need someone caring to carry us during the tough times of our lives; often it is the good Lord above.

He is there.
He's always near.
He hopes to help too.

Often, all you have to do is ask.
Often, all you have to do is love.
Often, all you need is a little hope.

Nothing goes unheard in his ears. He is always listening. However, his plans are not always our plans.

Lost in Your World:

March 17

Have you ever had a dream so nice you wish you could go back into it? And if you could, would you ever decide to come back if you were given the choice?

Being lost in the world of another can be pleasant from time to time. We all need a break, an escape from the humdrum. But sooner or later we must return to reality.

Being lost can be a blessing if instead of being afraid, you see it as an adventure.

Not knowing exactly where we're at can hone our senses of learning to go in the right direction. An inner sense of divine innocence often comes after being lost and finding yourself through humble self-discovery.

We're all lost at times. If anything, it finally makes us content to return home.

I Still Believe:

March 18

Belief is a beautiful thing. It's a reminder that things still matter. It offers hope.

On the flipside, if you believe in the wrong things, your direction in life can be misguided and lead you into poor choices that take you astray.

As we all struggle and strive for what matters most at any given moment, we should believe in *something*. Without it, we are adrift in a sea of changes.

Belief in things that bring spiritual soothing can make your mission crucial to our search for a heavenly home. It guides during difficult days and makes your faith strong and secure. It can help you reach your destination when sailing through rocky waters.

Our hearts, minds, and souls need belief.

What do *you* believe in?

Coming to Your Heart:
March 19

My dog had a heart murmur all the six years I had him. Then one night his heart started beating fast … much too fast.

It was the moment I knew his time was now. He had reached the end of a long journey.

And as sad as it was to have him put to sleep, when his body collapsed in my arms, his soul didn't leave yet. His spirit waited eight hours for me to prepare his soul for heaven. In that time, I did *everything* I could think of to make sure God knew to accept him.

During those eight hours, I sprinkled his body with holy water, rose petals, and extra ashes from Ash Wednesday. Another thing I did was get an extra sacramental communion wafer from church that morning and place it in his mouth. Finally, my single mother and I read Psalm 23 from the Bible with tears in our eyes before placing him in the grave I dug for him in his favorite resting spot in our yard.

I wanted to ensure he finally reached his true home after gracing my days for so long.

And even though paradise awaited his spirit's arrival, he delayed it until his funeral and final prayers were complete, and then his spirit spoke to my soul the following words: "Thank you, my eternal friend. I now see paradise, and I *will* see you on the other side."

His words, heard in my "voice of conscience," let me know that there *is* a heaven, and I hope that his journey there lets you know that we *all* have a heavenly home awaiting us.

Snuggling with the Silent Lucidity of Love: March 20

In the 1980s, the Seattle band Queensryche came out with a ballad called "Silent Lucidity." Its creation and distribution brought deep introspection to many people.

In it, it talks about achieving "dream control." Taken in the context of our sleep state, it offers amazing potential of what our minds can achieve. Taken in the form of what we do to make our desires a living and breathing reality, it offers much more.

We should never lose sight of our childhood dreams and aspirations.

Are you actively trying to make your altruistic dreams come true? If not, why?

For even if you only take a little bit of time each day to make them manifest reality, sooner or later you'll reach the other side of that long journey to achieve their perfection.

And even if that perfection never arrives, at least you will know that you did indeed try.

Sometimes that's all that really matters at the end of a long day or even after a long life.

We've All Lost Along the Way: March 21

When competitive pursuits are played, there is winning and losing at stake. A win brings prestige, pride, honors, accolades, and even the possibility of money. A loss brings some negative feelings, but it also offers a chance to learn which areas you're weak in.

A sporting coach once said about his favorite pastime, "The score is merely a time-keeping device. It simply indicates when the game begins and ends. What matters is that you truly are enjoying and savoring the activity of participation in the pursuit you love."

That little tidbit of Zen applies to more than just the games we watch or play, though. It applies to everything in life too. It's just how we perceive what we actively do.

Winning is nice, but it isn't everything.

Losing hurts, but it provides opportunity to learn.

Teach your children the benefits of both and watch them grow.

I'll Find You Someday:
March 22

What do you do to make "someday" a living reality? If that "someday" arrives today, will you be ready for it? Or will you even recognize it when it really comes?

This is where living each day as if it were your last can help guide your ways. If you live that way, you will be constantly asking yourself what matters most at this given moment. It offers inspiration to do important deeds during *this* day, then the next days as well.

If tomorrow never arrives, will you be content with the knowledge that you did all you could do to make the most of your current lot in life?

So think about making today the best it can be, but also make plans to ensure tomorrow will flow smoothly too. Then make it an everyday habit.

That "someday" *will* arrive if you constantly put practice into turning it into reality.

Sincerity and Truthfulness:
March 23

In searching the wine selection of a whole food market's vast collection of vino, I once came across a bottle with the name, *Sincerity*.

I smiled upon seeing it and bought it as a symbol. It was nice that it was organic too.

Isn't it amazing how a title and name can mean so much? It can represent what's inside, but it can also help us remember. And in that memory, there will exist a reminder of the truth that particular time in your life held.

Maybe that's why we name our babies, pets, and artistic creations.

Sincerity and truthfulness are good symbols in what they represent.

They're even better when they represent what we think, say, and do.

Add them to your daily repertoire!

I'll Give Anything to Hold You Tight: March 24

A tight hug that lasts more than just the ordinary greeting or goodbye says a lot about the person giving it, especially if it is done to show affection and tender loving care.

Each hug speaks volumes.

So often we encounter others who only offer a limp handshake or a weak hug. What do you think about their inner state of being when they greet you in this way?

In pondering that, think about teaching your children the importance of a firm handshake and giving a hearty hug, especially by setting the example yourself.

If you don't know how, make the time to learn. Then teach your kids the same.

If you do, you offer them a better chance of succeeding in life, for they mean so much.

First impressions begin with handshakes and hugs. Always put your best foot forward in order to excel.

Water's Refreshment:

March 25

In any given day, we all tend to drink a lot of fluids, and there are so many to choose from. Walk into any store, and you have a wide variety of choices: coffee, tea, soda pop, energy drinks, beer, wine, juice, milk ... and, of course, water.

They can energize, inebriate, replenish, and refresh.

However, since humans are mostly made up of water, always be aware of all the additives and calories each one adds to your body. They can have side-effects that take their toll as the years go by. It often pays to read the ingredients of what you ingest. For example, lots of carbonated beverages have plenty of chemicals that can damage your internal organs, and alcohol can definitely add some extra weight around your waistline.

But can you ever drink too much water?

It can clean the toxins your body builds up and refresh like no other drink can.

So think about getting into the habit of drinking more water on a daily basis and encouraging your kids to do the same. That habit may help you and your young ones stay healthier in the long run so you can all enjoy one another's love later on down the line.

Life in the Fast Lane:

March 26

Go too fast, and you may crash. Go too slow, and you may get bumped from behind. Go the right speed at the appropriate time, and you will reach your destination safely.

Also, if you travel at the correct velocity, you will arrive right on time.

The speed at which you travel is best when balanced with respect for your surroundings.

Don't be the slow car in the fast lane, and don't be the fast car in the slow lane, as that's how accidents occur. Awareness of our surroundings helps us bypass future mistakes.

Healthy Vegetarian Who Hikes:
March 27

Food is perhaps the most important drug we ingest daily. What we feed our bodies can either give the soul strength or empty weakness.

Combine a healthy diet with exercise such as hiking, and you'll be lean while seeing sights of nature that replenish the spirit.

If all you decide to eat are vegetables, you'll need patience for those who don't eat the same. If you date a vegetarian and crave meat once in a while, be open-minded.

We don't always see the same way on things.

That's what makes tolerance and consideration essential.

A balance of both helps in our humility and understanding of all.

Natural Paradise:

March 28

Nature offers a paradise unrivaled in many areas; however, the magnitude of this glory is amplified when within the pristine grandeur of any one of our national parks.

A national park is a place set aside in order to protect and preserve its natural beauty.

If you've never been to one, take the time to make it a destination soon. They revitalize.

If going to a national park requires a detour from your ordinary itinerary, try to decide to do so. If you do, you may create a remarkable memory to cherish the rest of your life. Also, remember to bring along a camera and use it often once there.

Later on, those snapshots of a special time in a special place will produce lasting smiles, refresh memories of good times gone past, and make you glad to be alive.

The Girl Next Door:
March 29

Our neighbors are important people. They can aid us when others aren't available.

If you are quarreling with a person nearby, making amends will produce peace of mind.

When someone new moves in, present him or her with a "welcome to the neighborhood" gift.

That fresh-baked cake you bring over to the new people next door may bring abundances. The people in the home next to you are the ones you'll typically see more often than others. When you pass them, wave and say hello. Stay on good terms.

The reward you receive will be the trust they return.

Strolling Main Street with a Skip in Our Step:

March 30

Main Street is a place that is usually the center of a city, town, or village. It is a place where people mingle, congregate, and gather.

Thus, if you do so by strolling or skipping it with another you care about, it can mean infinitely more than just walking that street alone.

When walking this city center together, try also to do it during days when festivals and fairs are in town. People watching alone is worth the trip, as will be the commentary you share while gazing at all the others. They *do* bring a wide variety.

Another option is to take that hand-in-hand stroll when all the street lamps are lit, because when they are, you'll notice things in a different way while sharing smiles.

Howl at the Moon with Me:

March 31

Seeing the full moon's glow rise over the horizon is such a nice sight. All the extra atmosphere at its original arrival makes it appear so much larger than when it is directly above. That larger appearance is a fleeting time, so if you see it, have another notice.

However, howling at the moon can be healthy too. That act can help release primal passions and tension that exist inside the animal within us all. If you've never mustered up the courage to howl at the moon, try it sometime. That howling may provide relief.

For example, my single mother's Red Hat Society chapter named themselves: W.O.L.F (Women of Laughter and Fun), and they start out each of their meeting *howling* for a moment. When they do, they all break out in good-natured giggles of glee that help them start their socializing on the right note.

Howling may offer some primal therapy that psychiatrists can't match. If we did indeed evolve from animals, allow that creature a little room to roam and be itself for a second. Howl!

April

No Medusa in the Mirror:

April 1

If the Spirit of God were to reveal your real-time inner truth in the mirror's reflection, what do you think you would see?

That distortion of your typical reflection, if done with complete truth, *could* encourage you to make much-needed changes in all you do and say.

It could give you the courage to stand tall, face yourself, and strive toward your destiny.

If "a mirror never lies" and if "God is truth," such a distortion of your reflection could encourage you to reach for all you ever dreamed to say, do, and become in this life.

Don't just dream about what you could be; make its arrival an active part of each day.

Where Eagles Dare:

April 2

During days long past, I wrote song lyrics called "Eagle" that go like this:

> Rising, flying, soaring, diving
> where only the eagles dare.
> Singing, swooping, mating, diving
> so majestic way up there.
>
> Calling, preying, dodging, darting
> flights of fancy fill their prayer.
> Rising, flying, soaring, diving
> with God's grace and love and flair!
>
> But, people, do you even see?
> I wonder if you really care.
> That out there in the far reaches of God's country
> there's really an eagle soaring out there!

So with my song lyrics in mind, try to take a bird-watching trip where your kids can see an eagle out in the wild. Its majesty will astound you!

Breakfast in Bed:

April 3

If someone you care about makes breakfast and brings it to you in your slumber, you may sense it in your sleep. Its aroma arouses. It awakens you into alertness and a new day.

If it's you who is doing the cooking in the other room, and others aren't up yet, isn't there a sense of joy you feel as you search for just the right ingredients that are pleasing to all?

That look on their faces as you bring them the unexpected meal is one that can linger all day and make your morning better than just the meal alone, as it's doing something special for others that makes you smile with an inner contentment.

Each meal you make is finite, but if you share it with others, the smiles become infinite.

Singing Solo, Looking for a Duet: April 4

When we sing together, our voices in unison produce a sweeter sound than singing alone, don't you think? And even if someone is a little off key, their contribution adds flavor simply because that person decided to participate rather than sit on the sideline.

This is especially poignant if you're singing solo. An addition that makes it a duet adds elements you couldn't have achieved alone, as loneliness usually welcomes any additional company, even if it doesn't lead to romantic desire.

A duet in anything you do contains a certain synergy too.

Shared harmony with syncopated rhythm can produce a sonnet that makes God smile.

How do you know when he is?

It's in the tingles in your soul.

Looks Good in Leather:
April 5

A purchase of a leather coat, a leather chair, or even leather boots and shoes is a special kind of "adult purchase." Its acquisition means you want to spend the extra money for its comfort, appearance, endurance, feel, texture, and comfort.

When you wear leather, it symbolizes durability and style.

Not only that, it speaks volumes about the person who purchased it.

Leather is a necessary luxury in the ascent into the realms of adulthood.

Therefore, when you purchase it for your teenagers, impress upon them the care they need to give their leather for it to last a lifetime.

Tease Me, Please Me, Just Don't Break My Heart:

April 6

When we're intimate with another, a barrier is broken. Those quiet and tender moments shared with one we truly care about means we are opening some of our deepest trust. That's when you might allow yourself to be more vulnerable than usual.

In those special times, we may playfully tease in order to please, yet once we break another's heart, all the fun and play instantly disappear, and seriousness sets in.

As a single mother, let your new mate know that your heart has already been broken once and for him to be aware of this fact so that he can proceed with extra-special care as your relationship unfolds.

Your tender warning may help him treat you with more delicacy about how his actions could end up breaking your heart once again. Thus, he might be more careful when it comes to testing your boundaries with careless teasing.

A Search for Soul:
April 7

We walk with tingles to an inner sense.
Goose bumps and shivers ... of divine innocence.

For only in listening do we learn how to hear.
For only then will God's voice be audible and oh
so clear.

Because if the door is open, a whisper will last.
But if the door is closed, indeed it will pass.

For the Lord uses a voice toward which we steer.
Yet, he uses a soft touch, which sends a single tear.

A tear of eternal knowing that he truly is "the one."
A tear of faithful reminder we *are* his daughters and
sons.

   With this poem in mind that I wrote years ago, keep
your senses open to God's loving care because he often
speaks to you internally if you're open enough to listen.

Is Honesty the Best Policy?

April 8

We've all been burned by being a little too open and honest.

As the saying goes, though, "The truth shall set you free."

Sticking to honesty is a habit that takes time to learn to do consistently. It is frequently very easy to let a little white lie slip through our lips.

If you make honesty a part of your everyday life, peace of mind will result simply because you're sticking to what actually occurred; therefore, if you're forced to recall a past incident later on, chances are you'll tell it as it actually happened.

Over time, white lies fade from memory, and only actual events are really recalled. Thus, teach yourself and your children to be truthful at all times because it's a habit that will serve you all very well in your later years. Also, though, once people *know* that you're trustworthy by having proved it in the past, your friendships will flourish.

Relaxing to Recharge Your Batteries:
April 9

What do you do as a single mother when you need to take a break in order to rest, recoup, and refresh yourself?

We all need time to take a few steps back so we can make a few leaps forward.

So perhaps you should arrange to have your kids stay with friends or family for a day or two so you can give yourself a breather from being a parent and recharge your battery in a variety of ways such as a bubble bath, a night out on the town with your girlfriends, or even a trip to a spa to pamper yourself.

A single mother tends to face a lot more stress than most people; therefore, give you and your frazzled nerves a break from the ordinary routine once in a while. The boost in your energy and refreshed outlook on life will make your kids happy you did.

Run the Race to the Finish Line:
April 10

In the marathon of life, it's easy to agonize over past faults. Each of our lives is filled with mistakes; and yet, that's where a healthy dose of forgiveness can help heal the wounds of old. Just as you hope others will pardon you, so should you forgive as well.

Absolution is a splendid thing. It provides a clean slate to work with—for all!

And as you journey through the years, there will be times when you stumble and fall. But even if you've fallen a thousand times, make sure to keep on getting up.

Because giving up silently acknowledges to yourself a sense of failure. Try and try again to find your finish line so that you inherently know the sensation of success. That elation of achieving your goal is one that provides self-respect and peace of mind. And those are feelings especially important to teach to your children for their future success.

Lay it on the Line:
April 11

Recognize the moment; do seize the day
before your fears keep you at bay.

Follow your bliss; do live your love
before your commitments crown like a glove.

Remember *carpe diem,* hip-hip hooray.
Dream another dream; do live for today

Journey out to the stars; lift your heart's love.
Spread your wings soon and fly like a dove.

Life is a Box of Chocolates:
April 12

If you've ever seen the Tom Hanks movie called *Forrest Gump*, you'll remember this day's title with a smile. It was advice on life that his momma gave him.

And even if you haven't, just imagine the variety of chocolates inside any given box.

There are so many different ones to choose from. And when you do, you're never really sure what will be on the inside. Often it's a choice that makes you savor and enjoy. Other times you may decide not to finish it, or you may set a few of them aside for someone else.

Regardless, each box of chocolates is usually received with a smile of not knowing how it will turn out when it is finished. Imagine receiving it to be like a baby being born. Then imagine finishing it to be like the end of your life. Each chocolate is a metaphor for what you do and what you create in life. Do you enjoy them all at once, or do you savor and share as many as possible to spread abundant joy into the world?

Open My Door and I'm Yours:
April 13

There's a song by the English progressive rock band Genesis called "Open Door." If you ever find it in a music store or online, take a listen.

It's kind of a sad and bittersweet song, but it also offers a sense of hope. All their songs provide inspiration in some way. Maybe that's why they were always my favorite.

It's a song that makes you think about times when a relationship comes to a close.

And yet, as long as the door is open there's still time to walk on through. There's still a chance the love can last. There's still a ray of light that beckons us inside.

Therefore, if someone holds a door open for you, smile and walk in with many thanks.

Is Chivalry Dead?

April 14

Every woman hopes a fine white knight will arrive to rescue her from her ivory tower. Likewise, every man dreams of being a knight in shining armor for a trapped princess. However, I often believe that a man must slay his own personal dragon in order to meet the maiden, win her love, and eventually marry her.

For a boy to become a chivalrous man, he must learn what it takes to conquer the dragon.

Most men have never fought this battle inside themselves, which is why I believe so many go through a midlife crisis around the age of forty. Then, their youth is really gone.

So if you're a single mom raising a son, teach him manners, dignity, and courage. The courage and discipline instilled in him will enable him to better face his own dragon. The manners and courtesy you teach your son will impress the eventual maiden he meets.

In Search of the Small, Simple Pleasures: April 15

Once, a recently married man expressed what it takes to make a marriage work: "Everything you do counts one. No matter how big or small the gesture, it counts one. A diamond means just as much as an unexpected rose. What counts is how many times you thought to do something for your spouse and not for yourself. As you build sweet gestures done for your wife, your union grows in appreciation and lasts all your life."

Therefore, remember that some of life's finer pleasures come in small packages.

What matters is that you try to be consistent in thinking of those you love—from the smallest gesture to the largest extravagance. This is a case where the quantity of times you look out for others can mean more than a mere one or two quality cases of concern. To think of your loved ones before you think of yourself is truly true love.

Will You Be My Photographer?
April 16

Photography is the essence of capturing a static snapshot of a dynamic moment in time. Everything included in that rectangle is what makes the photo.

Every photographer needs a pleasing model.
Every photo needs its rectangle to be as full as possible.
Every subject of each shot hopes to be captured in its best light.

The combined foreground and background of the main subject material separate a good photo from a great one that stands the test of time.

Few photos capture the true essence of what really existed in reality, as how can a two-dimensional snapshot fully describe three dimensions?

For the masterpiece photograph, someone is needed behind the shutter who sees and includes all layers of depth that can be contained.

If you find that person, make them yours; their photos will fill you with pleasure.

Hey, Adventure Spirit Pal:

April 17

The spirit of adventure is strong in someone you call a pal.

They are your sidekick.

They are your partner in all you do.

They are the one who is there in thick and thin.

During the good times, it is easy to be a friend; however, it's when times turn tough that you find out who your true friends are.

If you have a pal who has stuck by you even when all the chips were down, stay by him or her.

That person will be your trusted confidant. If you don't have a good friend you can tell your deepest secrets to, what's the good of the secret? Cherish your pal dearly.

Where Has My Social Life Gone?

April 18

For those who once had a busy social life and now find it a little lacking, rest easy.

A wise man once recalled as he was teaching class that after Beethoven finished writing a piece of music, he would go back through it and put in the silences.

Why would he do this?

He did it for the simple reason that spaces were what made the music flow.

So if you're currently in one of life's lulls, it just may be God giving the symphony of your life a little room to allow your music time and space to breathe.

I Have the Other Part of Your Heart: April 19

In my life, I've had many people who each have individual and unique pieces of my heart. Their influences produced a fulcrum effect that altered my life forever.

Is someone the same for you?

Did some soul start something in you too?

Was that particular person influential in your evolution?

If so, honor the day he or she was born. You may be miles apart physically, but if someone played a crucial role in your destiny, ask for him or her to have a special smile on his or her day.

That prayer you pray may get heard miles away.

Each one of us is made up of many.

Some are great; some are small.

Each had an influence.

Honor them.

Must Love Dogs and Life: April 20

April 20th is a day I will always remember, for it was the date my dog, Rebel, started having a heart attack, yet he remained his unconditionally loving self right to the end.

He was the one soul who truly taught me what love is. If you have a canine, I'm sure you understand. The degree of love and trust dogs bestow upon you is a gift from above.

If you have a dog and are looking to date, make sure that mate loves dogs just as much as you do, because your dog is like your child. And just as much as you wouldn't want someone who didn't appreciate your kids, you need someone who understands that your trusty canine companion means much more than any other animal.

Raised right, they are love.

Spell *dog* backwards ... what do you get?

God is love too.

Looking Forward to the Future:
April 21

The future is an interesting destination. It's always unknown, yet it can be forecast. How? By making consistent preparations for it, for then it can become a blessing.

Planning for the future gives us something to look forward to and provides hope.

Hope for reaching that next day is what keeps us fresh and alive inside.

For those who aren't concerned about the future, it may be tough.

Life works best as we persevere to earn tomorrow's prosperity.

Remember, "Luck is when opportunity meets preparation."

A Woman Who Knows What She Wants: April 22

A single mom who knows what she wants is a very finicky soul indeed. She's not one who has the wool pulled over her eyes easily.

Since single moms have seen it all already, nothing much surprises them.

People with worldly experience have seen so much that they pretty much know what their type is when it comes to romance. When they find it, they run to it.

However, when you see someone who fits the description of what you want, be cautious. Physical appearances can be deceiving. They only go skin deep.

As the saying goes, "Be careful what you wish for; you just might get it."

Truer words were never spoken.

Frontiers of Travel and Adventure:

April 23

Traveling the world provides perspective on the texture of different cultures and diversity. It encourages a humble and compassionate outlook on life.

Also, it enables an ability to see what our earth holds.

That travel can help hone your sense of what you're looking for in love.

Being that you see so many people in a variety of cultural ties, you occasionally see traits that stand out and resonate. Something about them speaks volumes to your passions.

When you find that person who rings the bell inside your heart, put your best foot forward. Then explore the adventures that await with open arms.

True Compassion Wanted:

April 24

A relationship with even the truest companion is never easy. Things always happen to rub the other the wrong way. It's inevitable. You've gotta roll with the changes.

In cases where an error occurs in how we anticipate our companion's time schedule to fit into ours, frustration occasionally sets in.

It's how we face these rough spots that make the difference. Being united to keep the relationship at its best is what determines the ultimate length of your union.

We all get a little selfish with our time, and if we want our companion in our life, we have to learn to apologize frequently and with a sincere heart.

The more often each of you is compassionate to your mutual needs, the better the glue holds.

I've Been to the Puppet Show: April 25

Puppet shows are a great place to present your kids with easy-to-understand metaphors for the realities that lie ahead of them. They teach in unique ways.

So if you take your kids to go see puppets perform, always make sure to challenge them to explain the lessons they learned after they witnessed the show. If anything, it may provide some unique perspectives that enable you all to learn new lessons.

Also, though, it encourages communication within your family.

And just as a family that prays together stays together, families who keep the lines of communication open in all circumstances tend to be close lifelong friends.

Therefore, teach your kids to talk out their troubles ... even if they have to use a puppet to do so. It may allow them the courage to say the things truly on their mind.

Missing Element to Happiness:
April 26

In quantum physics, there's a concept known as the uncertainty principle. Basically, it boils down to the fact that nature, at its subatomic level, tends to hide and be elusive. If you know one thing about a small particle, you won't know its other prime characteristic. Vice versa, if you know the missing element, the other thing you knew previously now suddenly becomes elusive.

In other words, sometimes God hides.

The same is true with human characteristics and interactions.

If you have financial security, you may be searching for happiness. If you have love and joy, material abundance may be the element you're still missing.

It's always something, yet that's the spice of life.

Remember that life will always have some guesswork involved ... even when we think we know it all.

The Heroism of a Mother:

April 27

Mothers have to be amongst the most heroic of all God's creatures … especially single mothers. This is because they tend to teach, listen to, and love their kids throughout their entire lives. The bond that starts in the womb is life-long.

Thus, when heavenly medals are awarded in eternity, mothers must earn the most.

The struggles they face start in pregnancy; and yet, it's a hero's path they proceed upon with courage, stamina, and endurance.

So up in heaven, who do you think God would give the gold medal to if their souls were to stand side-by-side? The Olympic athlete who set a world record, or the mom who loved her kids all her life and propelled her children toward prosperity?

The Great Outdoors:
April 28

Share a love of the great outdoors with your kids. As they grow with this love, their attention to nature's details may be eye-opening once they learn to see its subtleties.

They'll teach you to appreciate the day when the sunset and moonrise are simultaneous.

Likewise, they'll be the ones to wake you up in order to see a meteor shower at night.

Other times, they may have you walk outside to see a lunar eclipse in the sky.

The moments of God's greatest grandeur outdoors are fleeting times, and only an aware few truly take the time to pause and savor every second.

And though they'll always have their hidden faults and shortcomings, as everyone does, they'll help guide you to learn how to stop, drop all you're doing, and make the most of the greatest art gallery in the world—Mother Nature—when she is at her best.

Kids are keenly aware of details you may miss on your own; thus, teach them to love the great outdoors at an early age so they can keep filling you up outside and in.

Sweet and Sassy:

April 29

A little sass with class goes a long way to add interesting ingredients to any relationship.

Too much sass overpowers your dish of love.

Too little makes your union bland and boring.

That's where it's nice to blend your recipe for desire with a generous mixture of sweets.

The balance between the two is like a cook in the kitchen who has to learn not to overcook or undercook any meal, often through trial and error.

Practice makes perfect.

The moral here is to balance all your best traits so that their blend never becomes a burden to the ones you love.

Miss Independent:
April 30

Independence is a beautiful quality to possess. It allows freedom of choice, freedom of thought, freedom of speech, and freedom of honest actions.

However, independence needs the essence of some sense of structure.

Too much freedom can lead to wild and out-of-control actions.

Total independence can soon turn into aching loneliness.

Being a "Miss Independent" or "Mister Independent" can blind us from realizing that we all live on the planet in a state of coexistence in which we tend to need one another.

Don't be afraid to be dependent once in a while. Another's thoughtful action *is* a blessing.

May

Sick of Frogs... Where is My Prince?

May 1

Each young lady sort of fashions herself as a princess who must kiss a lot of frogs before she finds her prince. Yet, if you've seen yourself this way, as a single mom, it may become a little tiresome to keep kissing frogs.

However, even all the frogs can teach you a thing or two along the way. For example, perhaps they help you learn to leap from lily pad to shore in order to avoid sinking and to find solid ground. In other words, each frog has a lesson to learn from.

The imperfections of humanity *do* lead to a lot of let-downs.

But if you keep trying to find love, it may arrive when you least expect it.

Even Thomas Edison made a lot of faulty light bulbs before he found one that finally worked. Each error he made helped him arrive at the successful solution.

The same should apply to you as you look for love amongst the lily pads of life.

Godiva Chocolates Only ... Please:
May 2

When making a day trip to the mall, if you have any extra money, try to stop in the Godiva store. Even if you only have spare change to buy one chocolate, its quality will make you smile and be glad you stopped in to treat yourself.

Often an extravagant gesture you do for yourself will fill you up in unexpected ways. Maybe later you'll share such fine quality with another who hasn't had the same experience. Or maybe you'll purchase something that brings a finer degree of comfort for a soul in obvious distress or pain; believe me, your gesture makes a difference.

If you learn the degrees of quality that surround us via earned experience, at some point there will come a time when you want to share that inherent wisdom with another, which enables that person to expand his or her horizon and brighten their day.

That person's pleasure will then be your delight!

This Should Be Fun:

May 3

What is the definition of fun?

Even tedious tasks can turn fun when looked at with the proper perspective. Perhaps it's what you incorporate into other people as you do your daily deeds. At times it becomes something you need to set aside to come back to with a fresh mind. It can also be driving down a scenic road you've never been down before.

The one thing to keep in mind is to try to possess a child's zest in all that comes your way because when you do, the essence of fun somehow tends to seep in.

That child's newness can make even an ordinary task much more enjoyable.

Try to include it in each day.

Ambitious Woman:

May 4

Ambition is a beautiful sense of drive. It enables us to focus. Important desires come to the forefront and are a motivating force in how we proceed.

It's interesting, though. Initial ambitions are necessary to set a dream in motion in order to become a reality, but once it becomes work, do you possess the sense of duty, drive, and perseverance to see it through to proper completion?

And once you do complete it, another boost of ambition is needed for the *next* dream. That takes time to refresh and refill your heart and mind in order to regain the gumption.

Remember to take time in between activities in order to restore your ambition.

Even God took a day to rest on the seventh day.

So should you!

Passionate by Nature! Romantic by Desire!

May 5

Today's title contains two exclamation marks simply because the words within each short phrase often demand and require them.

Passion, for instance, is a strong emotion. Romance is one of the true blessings of humanity. Nature often contains infinite variety. Desire seems to fuel our actions.

Combining them all together to describe yourself means your essential being is alive inside with a flame in your heart that will never be extinguished if you stay strong.

Some people are so tame and docile that all their statements end in periods. Others are so full of energy that they require exclamation points to end everything they say and do.

Ask yourself how often your words form sentences that need more than a simple period. Therefore, lead a life that demands lots of exclamation points to describe!

Live, Laugh, Learn, Love:

May 6

For today, please think about how much time you spend with your children. Are their emotional and spiritual demands being met by you?

In listening to a pastor elaborate on the confessions he heard from young ones, he emphasized that their prime concern was that they wanted more quality time with their parents. They expressed that even though they could be in the same room as a parent, quality communication and listening were seriously lacking.

Some were starving for more together time with Mom or Dad.

With this said, in order to enable your children to live, learn, laugh, and love as adults, more quality time may be needed from you today.

It's something to ponder while you do things for yourself each day.

Make Me Laugh Out Loud:
May 7

Do you have someone in your life who can tell a great joke? Has that person ever made you laugh so hard you spit out your drink? Can he or she bring the sort of loud laughter that requires a snort or even makes you gasp for air after the joke or funny story is told?

If you have such a person who can make you laugh like that, stay on good terms with him or her and let them know how much you do care for the way they make you laugh. If they can produce such an effect on you that brings wide smiles later on when you truly need it, they are to be cherished indeed.

Even in dire times, a great belly laugh can help us set all our worries aside. If that laughing out loud comes to you, don't hold it back! It's good for your soul to let it out.

Who knows, you may need it more than you think.

Hang On and Enjoy the Ride:
May 8

When the one you love says, "I love you" without an "if" or "when," isn't it a wonderful thing to hear and receive? Doesn't it make you feel oh so special? Like magic?

This is especially the case when it's the first time he says it.

When the first "I love you" slips from his lips, a part of your heart leaps with joy because you now know that the relationship has gone to that next level.

When it occurs, a part of you prepares because it's time to hang on and enjoy the ride of love and life. The two of you are now embarking upon something serious. And while it can be a rollercoaster ride with lots of twists and turns, the exhilarating rush you feel while riding it is beyond belief and comprehension. It can be eternally everlasting.

Hoping for My Last First Date: May 9

First dates can be fun. There is a lot of anticipation for the potential offered in each one. Then the first rendezvous occurs, and you finally see each other.

In that first sighting of each other, much goes on in the minds of both parties. Each one's imagined bubble of fantasy either bursts or balloons. Reality is then realized.

One thing to think about in the midst of many first dates is your children's feelings through all these ordeals you are experiencing.

If you bring a string of men into your home, how will they know a sense of permanence in terms of a male role model?

Also, many males marching in may produce confusion in their spirit and soul.

Always look before you leap into a romance.

Think of your children too.

Friends First, Computer Last:

May 10

I know a wonderful woman who goes to the bar many nights a week to drink herself silly because her husband comes home from work, goes to his den, and sits on the computer all evening instead of spending his home time with her and his children.

He provides well for his family financially. He makes sure all basic needs are satisfied. However, he often forgets he has a wife who longs for his love.

She suffers because of his fascination with the virtual world of the computer's artificial reality. Her growing alcoholism is a direct effect of the addictive nature of the Internet.

Her loneliness is obvious as she sits at the end of the bar month after month.

If you have a second chance at new love, choose your mate with wisdom.

Make sure he realizes that you come first and his computer comes last.

Mean What You Say and Say What You Mean:

May 11

How many people do you know who actually and literally "walk the walk" after they "talk the talk"? This sort of person tends to be rare, so cherish him or her.

Isn't it frustrating when you encounter someone who says they'll be there in a few minutes, and then they show up a half hour later?

These types of exaggerations only cause frustration and resentment in others.

If you happen to be the type of person who doesn't do what you say you will, make vast strides to change this behavior as immediately as possible. If you say something, take an active role in ensuring that you follow through.

Life flows and trust lasts when you do what you say and say what you mean.

Quality Girl Seeking a Guy with Class: May 12

For the single mom who contains a fine degree of quality, finding a guy with class is a must. Others just don't seem to satisfy as much.

If anything, you're the one who takes the extra care to see that your children receive a fantastic education for future success in life. You make sure they do their homework.

For a single mom with quality, since you take the time to get all the details right, you don't want a mate who couldn't care less. You need a man who opens doors for you and helps you with your coat. You desire and deserve a gentleman. When you find him, watch the sparks fly!

Smart, Sexy, and Sassy Seeks Same:
May 13

When a baby is born, maturity is mandatory. It doesn't stop at the end of our teenage years either. If anything, it becomes a greater necessity. Maturity always continues on.

If maturity has made you smarter, sexier, and even a little sassier, chances are you won't be satisfied with a mate who doesn't possess the same qualities.

Chutzpah holds itself strong in these qualities.

Strive for that extra lesson to learn quickly.

Perspective from experience is a blessing.

A sexy and sassy woman will attract many men. If she's smart enough to balance them with ease, the more mature males will take notice. They've seen the wannabes and want a real woman, not some little girl who gets caught up in materialism.

Be that mature woman for him and for your children.

They all *will* adore you.

Stay by Me:
May 14

Singer Annie Lennox sings a gorgeously sensuous song called "Stay by Me," which is on her CD entitled "Diva." If you don't have this release, I strongly encourage you to pick it up, especially if you possess a passion for romance. It will not disappoint.

Her soulful singing and soothing compositions on that CD can help your cares drift away.

The last half of the songs on that release are fertile soil for setting a romantic mood with the one you love. Also, her voice is simply a gift from God and a blessing to hear.

Finally, when you play that CD with someone special, make sure the lights are low. Light a few candles and listen with a nice beverage. You will appreciate it.

A Talent for Introspection:

May 15

Fantasies of the mind provide an interesting sense of introspection, and so do the quiet storms we all must weather and pass through in our journeys.

Within all facets of life, time for introspection is a vital essential. Those deep internal thoughts help process the past events and put them into their proper perspective.

Even after initial introspection, time away is needed to see with fresh hindsight.

Analyzing an event in the moment and after time's passage allows us to see something from all sides, with wisdom and insight as the results.

Saving the Best for Last:
May 16

When writing a paper, what's best? Your first draft or your last proofread draft, having had lots of people read initial drafts and provide constructive criticism?

So many obstacles must be cleared in order to reach a finished product. So much work must be done from initial inspiration to create the completed masterpiece.

However, with practice and perseverance, perfection can be achieved.

The thing to remember is that you should never give up. You may need to set your pursuit aside in order to return to it with a fresh perspective, but once you rejoin the race to the finish line, you do so with a renewed sense of inspiration.

Keep your head held high and keep on keeping on. The best is yet to come!

Care for a Bubble Bath?

May 17

A bath with bubbles is better than one with just water alone. If anything, the ability to hide and play with the foaming suds can lead to exploration. Don't be frugal on the bubbles either; if anything, add more.

A bath is far different from a shower too. One is typically quick and done standing up. The other requires time to draw the water, add the bubbles, and ease in slowly.

Also, a bath encourages taking time to scrub, time to let the water soak in, and of course, time to sit, relax, and let the introspection flow as the worries drift away.

And oh yeah, a squeaky rubber ducky can add a few delightful laughs along the way!

Missing Sensuality:
May 18

Sensuality is like a fine red wine. It gets better with age. Courage to explore increases as we age, ripen, and mature.

Even if you're a single mother who hasn't had romance in a while, that doesn't mean that the sensual side of yourself needs to get lost. If anything, it can still grow by the way you treat yourself and others with class, dignity, and style.

So often I see single moms who stick to the same old routine day-in and day-out.

I know, because I occasionally get stuck in that same rut.

That's where getting dressed up and putting on all your make-up in order to treat yourself to something special is occasionally needed. Because when you take the time to feel special, others will treat you special as well. It may even cause you to stroll instead of the typical bustling about.

Many times, dressing up feels like wearing a costume or a suit of armor, and the air with which you wear it makes others take notice … often with an air of refreshment that you need for rejuvenation.

Snuggling Under the Stars:
May 19

Pushing the boundaries of sight is ultimately what it means to look across an ocean or into the nighttime sky on a cloudless night.

Spotting constellations, an aurora, a passing satellite, or even a shooting star provides a sense that the sky is constantly changing and oh so dynamic.

Looking at a certain star early in the evening and then late at night will show you it has changed position with the earth's rotation.

Even more is when you speak a profound thought and see a shooting star streak across the sky. Is it coincidence, destiny, or God letting you know he heard your cry?

Regardless, time together spent snuggling outside is always very special. And it doesn't just have to be with a lover. It just as easily can be with your kids too!

Savoring All the Seasons:

May 20

The change of seasons from winter to spring brings about a refreshed sense of spirit and a renewed mentality to tackle the next set of tasks on your agenda.

It's hard not to feel this way when all the flowers are sprouting and blossoming. Also, the birds all seem so vibrant. Watching their young ones flutter their wings may bring a smile when they're trying to get their parents to share some of the food they've gathered.

Yet all seasons have their special, cherished, and unique characteristics. Pristine snowfall, while so far away in May, has its moment of appreciation when it does indeed finally arrive. With spring in full swing, it's time to savor the birds, the bees, and love.

Ripples of Reality Soar through My Soul: May 21

When a pebble is thrown into the water, it creates a ripple that settles down over time and distance, much like our emotions.

Try to think of any event as having an emotional impact that ripples in your psyche. The closer you are to a source event, the stronger the waves will be as well.

For example, when someone you love passes away, the initial ripple is strongest. The grief makes the ripples seem like tidal waves. Then as time goes on, the feelings subside, we cope with our grief, and the moving-on part begins.

When the initial wave hits, it's important to realize how strong the waves are that it creates and proceed onward with the knowledge that time eases these emotions.

Love the Feel of Family:

May 22

Mother Theresa once said, "If you are full of love, you are full of joy."

Also important are wisdom and common sense. These are like feathers in your cap. Giving them all— love, joy, wisdom, common sense—to your children is a goal.

For the family that distributes them freely, there is a firm foundation that lasts. The permanence of their possession not only lasts life-long, but it lasts eternally as well. When we integrate them into our psyche, they get differentiated out of us naturally with abundance, presence, and impact in what we do and in what we create.

People perpetuating these traits are like multifaceted gems. They shine forth from all angles, from each family, filled with their loving and giving gifts.

A Phoenix Out of the Ashes:

May 23

Taking the chance to pass through the boundaries of failure is what sums up the story of the mighty phoenix rising out of the ashes.

So many times, standing on a platform of victory arrives after so many defeats.

Out of the inevitable dust cloud that ashes create, we *can* rise again.

I often wonder what went through the phoenix's mind after its rebirth. It passed through a moment of death to once again fly free and alive. Its knowing there *is* life after death provides continual courage each and every time it soars again; for once we fail, we know that there's no place to go but up. Become reborn in your belief, hope, and love.

Strive to rise again and again …

Tired of Swimming with Sharks:

May 24

Would you consider yourself a shark or a dolphin if you were given the choice between the two? Whereas dolphins are typically smarter and friendlier, sharks still swim the waters wherever we go, prowling for new prey, a lurking danger to the unaware.

When you're surrounded by sharks, it becomes necessary either to be like one of them or just get out of the water in the first place.

The deeper the water of life you swim within, the more the sharks prowl. For this reason, some of us never go out into the ocean. However, when you ride the waves, be aware.

Knowing the surroundings *can* pay dividends.

It can save your life when danger lurks.

Learn to sense the dolphins and sharks.

Because in the seas of life, some people you encounter will be dolphins coming to the rescue, and others will be sharks looking to devour. Thus, always pay attention so you can spot one from the other in everything you do.

Bread and Roses:

May 25

"Bread and Roses" was the name of a place that served fresh meals to the homeless, where they were seated and served by volunteers who waited the tables, provided a small list of breakfast choices, and then brought them their food with a smile.

It was a way to provide some small sense of dignity to the less fortunate.

There was a flower in a vase sitting upon each table, and by having them assigned to random seats, they always had new company with which to share fresh conversation.

Finally, the guests were permitted to take a flower with them in hopes that the natural beauty would brighten their day by carrying it around for the whole world to see.

Therefore, never be afraid to help a homeless soul smell and feel like a rose.

Seeing a Sunset off the Reflections of Your Eyes:
May 26

Ponce de León's "fountain of youth" was a fantastic hope that kept him searching for a way to stay young forever.

If you ever found such a fountain of youth, would you really want to take a drink?

Consider the possibility that doing so could rob you of many memories and wisdom.

Think about all the sunsets you witnessed in the arms of a dear lover. If you drank that youthful elixir, would you still remember seeing sights of beauty in the eyes of another?

Those cherished memories took time, age, and experience to create.

Your maturity is more valuable than you may think!

Exploration and Adventure:

May 27

Exploring anywhere new with the one you love leads your souls into many adventures.

A whole lotta love with a little boogie in your shared steps causes these new lands to take on special meaning that can lead to later conversations that illuminate all sides of the experience each of you witnessed, kind of like the Indians would do after an event.

While you may have noticed certain specific details, your companion probably noticed others. And in communicating those individual perceptions, the moment indeed echoes and grows.

What your friend recalls may make you quiver with appreciation of having him by your side, helping to point out the things you may have missed or ignored.

Synergy, exploration, and adventure—wonderful things indeed.

Seeking Sun, Standing in Rain: May 28

Someone who is standing in the rain and hoping for sunshine needs a little tender loving care. That TLC can soak through much easier than a simple raindrop. The care penetrates into our inner being and makes standing in the rain so much nicer.

It's interesting, though. Sometimes when days of rain add up, we look for sun.

When we're in the midst of a long dry spell, a little rain replenishes nicely.

Too much heat requires cooling.

A lot of cold desires warmth.

It's all about the balance.

Even when the weather is right, all can be wrong inside.

Even when the conditions require change, smiles can still abound.

With love in your heart and hope in your soul, all will work out in time.

Loving, Touching, Squeezing:
May 29

For many of us, today's title may remind you of the song by the band Journey.

When you combine them all together—loving and touching and squeezing—you feel the spirit soaring through your body, mind, and soul.

Loving touches and squeezes let the recipient know the gentle heart that beats within. They show a gentle nature filled with genuine care and concern.

When given with truth and honesty, they linger and last. As they are given back, they form an upward spiral with others that lingers and radiates to all. Those loving echoes form an aura of love, care, honor, and trust that others *do* and *will* notice daily.

Give them freely; they *will* return your investment.

Tales of a Bikini Bartender:

May 30

Do you have beautiful young daughter approaching maturity? Is her appearance exceptional? Does she make men turn their heads toward her as she passes?

If so, teach her to avoid the easy trap of quick-cash job opportunities.

Two such easy opportunities for a beautiful young lady are that of a stripper and bikini bartender and/or lingerie waitress. Each one is a trap you should help her avoid if at all possible. Why? Simply because they are establishments that will cause her to sell a small piece of her soul so men can watch and ogle her for quick and dirty tips of cash. The money may be fast and easy, but the cost is selling out her mind for money.

Beauty fades with age. An addiction to fast cash sells the soul. Avoid them early and teach your daughters to do the same.

Have My Eye on the Pie:
May 31

Our eyes are amazing creations.

Sometimes they are looking up.

Other times they look downward.

Each new sight hopes for delight.

The eyes reveal so much too!

Watch a person's eyes, and you know much.

They truly are the windows to our heart and soul.

An eye seeing the sights of nature dances with delight.

An eye on the pie keeps perseverance and focus.

An eye gazing on God sees utter beauty.

What you allow your eyes to see over a lifetime determines your peace of mind.

Guide your eyes to life's good things and watch the blessings become abundant!

June

I Know How to Treat You Right:
June 1

Have you ever stepped outside on an early morning and let the sky's perfect colors soak through your spirit and soul? If you have, it fills you unlike at other times during the day. Those early colors are magic. They possess a quality only God can produce.

It's as if the Lord knows how to treat all the early-risers right, yet how many notice?

In treating each other the right way, it's important to think of your loved ones … such as your children and parents.

Try to think of how they feel before you make any important actions.

Any alarms you hear or feel should always be acknowledged; and yet, altruistic actions often are necessary to keep your most special bonds solid and strong.

First-class treatment toward each other reaps rewards that last into eternity!

Some Kind of Wonderful:

June 2

Internet dating is different from when we see someone in our presence that makes cupid shoot his arrow of Eros straight through our heart.

Love at first sight is some kind of wonderful. It stirs a desire and drive to keep that love beating in our heart, for that person in our midst may be "the one" to keep us alive.

It's unmistakable too.

However, when we Internet date, we fall in love with a picture, shared e-mails, instant messaging communications, and telephone calls, with a meeting later down the line.

It's not the same instant spark as love at first sight. Instead, it's a slow flame.

One flame burns bright. The other warms with time.

They're different, but both are still wonderful.

Hold on Loosely, But Don't Let Go:
June 3

Today's title comes from the 38 Special song of the same name, but it reveals an essential truth to help make relationships last. We need to have time to be our uncensored self. We desire space to be with other friends as well.

Too much time together can set each other on edge. As the saying goes, "Familiarity breeds contempt." So true that saying is.

If we're always in the same place together, it's easy to get on each other's nerves. We all need room to grow and breathe. Space helps the heart grow fonder.

Yet, a long leash on each other doesn't mean letting go either. If anything, the room to roam only brings back great tales to share with our special someone when we return to those loving arms around us, which we missed while we were away.

Let's Watch the Butterflies Flutter By:

June 4

Have you ever gone into a butterfly sanctuary? If you haven't, it's really a delight beyond explanation alone. You have to be inside one to truly understand. It's such a surreal experience, one you'll never forget.

One blustery winter day in the midst of a raging snowstorm, traffic was so jammed on the highways that I exited the nearest off-ramp in Detroit only to find myself in front of the Detroit Zoo. Curiosity and time on my hands led me to see if it was open. It was!

So, dressed warmly, I wandered in and was one of only a very few people inside. After serenading a group of snow-covered camels with my drumstick percussion skills, I saw a lighted building, walked inside many moisture-sealed doors, and found myself in a tropical butterfly sanctuary. What a dichotomy! Going from subzero snow to humid heat and butterflies fluttering past my eyes was a delight I still thank God for every day!

Thus, think about taking your kids to the zoo one day and hope that they have a butterfly sanctuary ... especially if it's at the time when they emerge from their cocoons!

Meet Me Halfway:

June 5

If you stay at home a little too often, you might learn to realize that the walls close in.

That's where getting out and about is necessary. Time to stretch your wings and soar every once in a while is necessary for mental stability and sanity.

If you have a long-distance friend, offer to meet him or her halfway. Your friend may appreciate your earnest sincerity in caring to see them and rendezvous in the middle.

Times like those are rare, but taking a trip out of the ordinary to visit with an old friend is like a breath of fresh air. Since time has passed since you two last saw each other, you'll both notice changes. But in reminiscing over old times, you'll return to the ordinary routine with a renewal of energy, smiles, and joy to keep on keeping on.

Tell Me Sweet Nothings at Night:
June 6

A sweet nothing at night can mean so much when said the right way. Often, it tends to be the tone in our voice when heard. If done with a teasing nibble on the earlobe or a soft caress, it can turn into a passionate desire that brings pleasure to both.

Also, knowing that that person isn't going to leave in the middle of the night is reassuring. Because if he stays, you have the delight of knowing your bed won't be empty in the morning. That feeling is definitely reassuring to our souls as well.

Hearing those sweet nothings at night is nice, but they're even better when they are coupled with sharing plans for the next day together.

Those sweet sayings shouldn't have an agenda either.
They should just be meant to make you smile.
That's when they are at their absolute best.

Sharing Stories over Smiles:

June 7

Storytelling, both verbal and nonverbal, is a way in which we share experiences with others. We do it to express an inner need to communicate our wisdom with any and all.

This is especially important for children. We need to help their young minds realize how large a world there is out there for them. Often, they will imagine the settings and environment as well as the details of each character. If they were all to translate what they envisioned in their minds in an artistic sense, there would be many interpretations.

Each translation of any story has its own view of important points that need emphasis. However, when they are all looked at as a whole, they form a multifaceted gem of the truth that captures their story in its full essence, a gem that shines oh so brightly!

88 Keys to Win the Way to My Heart: June 8

Playing a piano produces productive passion. Striking a single key makes it resonate sweetly.

And while playing the right notes and chords with precision is usually more appreciated, sometimes a unique player causes our ear to yearn for more. They may play differently than most practiced players, but their unique style will never be forgotten.

And isn't that what God wants?

The way we play might not reproduce Beethoven, Mozart, or Bach, but your unique contribution while tickling the ivories will be heard ... if only for an audience of one.

Because when the Lord hears you produce something truly new, his ear *does* take notice.

Hearing the Rhythms of Life:
June 9

Is someone you know with a rhythmic talent searching for a way to express it more actively? If so, one way to pursue this is to encourage him or her to practice daily. Even if you've never uncovered your musical talents, it's never too late to start.

One of the greatest lessons I ever learned was that you don't necessarily need an instrument to hone the talent of your own rhythm, as often, allowing your fingers, feet, and body to follow the beat may lead to days of dancing in your seat.

Much of my own musical practice never takes place with an instrument in front of me. Many times I just allow my toes to tap or fingers to follow the notes with my style.

Then when I play with an actual musical instrument, all that muscle memory of following every tune just flows naturally, and musical talent never grows old.

Save a Horse, Ride a Cowboy:
June 10

Today's title is from a popular country song.

Tongue in cheek, its satire lingers with a smile.

In today's times, true cowboys are a dying breed, as are the women who appreciate their rugged ways. Today, in a city setting, they *do* stand out. Their cowboy hat gives them away, and if they're brave enough to have long hair and wear spurs in public, it definitely puts the policeman with an ultra-short haircut on edge.

However, there's a certain code of honor and dignity within a cowboy that most do not possess. Cowboys are the type to make a tough decision in dire situations, one that hopes to save as many souls as possible.

These honorable intentions especially apply to women and children.

And while the cowboy may be a little rugged around the edges, if you find and love one, hold on, love him dearly, and always enjoy the ride.

Fairytale Timing:

June 11

Do you ever wonder what happens to all your favorite fairytale characters after their story comes to an end? Similarly, what happens when the honeymoon ends for the prince and the princess? Do their roll up their sleeves and get to work loving each other?

Every fairy tale has an ending.

It's not always as we see in the movies either.

However, we do create our own individual reality.

If the fairy tale has evaporated into mere reality, it's time to make the most of the small blessings each day brings. We can all fall into a hole or a rut sometimes.

But that's where serendipity may bring a blessed soul to soothe a sad day.

If so, honor that blessing-bringing person in a special way.

The timing of their arrival may be what you need!

A Queen in Search of Her King:
June 12

As yesterday's theme was about fairytales, such as princes and princesses, I often wonder what it takes for them to turn into a king and a queen who rule their kingdom.

And I feel that the answer is often age, experience, and maturity.

When we're young, it's so easy to ignore the realities of today's society.

When we're older, we start to see all the respective angles ... often all too well.

Each day holds a vast array of experiences.

And it is up to you to make today a good day.

If it seems impossible to do so, try with zest anyway.

You never know what today holds. Perhaps you will be a beautiful queen to the courtly king who has been searching for you all his life.

Strumming Your Way to My Heart:
June 13

The resonation of strings being strummed the right way is a blessed sound to hear. That right note played with passion can cause a concatenation of joy that echoes.

Your glee can give a smile to the next one you meet, which gets passed along to infinity.

Plucking a string produces a vibration that sets a radiation into the air for all to hear and feel. That resonation of one single string can make hearts flutter and spirits soar. If you feel that, let it flow through you. Then allow it to ripple and roar with waves that soar because one note *can* change the whole world.

Still Feeling Like a Kid at Heart:
June 14

A sense of reckless abandon is needed and necessary to still feel young every once in a while. As we age, this resonation of the youthful feeling has its time and place.

Acting silly, cracking bad jokes that cause groans, and being willing to stand naked in front of a crowd are all attributes of the essence of youth.

Never feel afraid to let yourself go in a moment when you're around friends. That act of not caring what others may think often produces a silent smile when it really matters.

Times of heartbreak, grief, or sorrow need a lift of spirits. Acting like a kid again can regain that lift your soul needs to move on. Give it a try. What do you have to lose?

With Hope Still Shining in My Eyes: June 15

Hope is a strange creature. It permits positive feelings to flow freely. It is also often shunned by the many we may encounter.

If hope still shines in your eyes, never let it go! Don't let another rain all over your parade. Let your love flow freely with an awesome abundance to all others.

Our faith, hope, and belief in all that is good and just is what makes the United States of America special. And while other countries possess those traits too, it seems to flourish in the good ol' USA.

If you encounter someone who has lost the shine in their eyes, don't let his or her dull glow diminish what radiates from within your heart and soul.

The hope you give is the hope you will eventually receive.

Pass it along to your children and others as well!

Seeking Sparks:

June 16

The spark of life begins in the womb. There, something mystical and magical occurs, which allows a man and woman to create life. And what a creation it is!

Some may think that that spark is unimportant. And although it may get snuffed out too soon, the fact remains that a new life *did* exist. It did begin. It did love.

Love always exists in each new life. Though it may only cautiously surface, it matters.

Therefore, if you are a new mother considering your new child, just think of all the minor miracles it may cause or witness later in its life. It may be there when you need it.

When you think this way, you will be grateful you allowed it to flourish with your nurturing and nourishment. Each life deserves a chance to love and grow.

Hoping to Feel the Inebriation of Love and Desire:

June 17

How we perceive different sorts of inebriation is an interesting thing, and some people seem to want us to feel as though we're somehow not achieving our full potential if we partake.

Life is tough. We're all hurting one way or another.

And by inebriation, I'm not just referring to alcohol. There are many ways we escape. Some overindulge in food. Another escape we can get carried away with is the Internet. Another is prescription painkillers, and of course, there are things such as alcohol and illegal drugs that some use to take the edge off of a difficult day in a less-approved way.

Those escapes enable us to cope. Some are legal; some are not. However, if they manage to recharge our best attributes, are they bad?

We all have our own form of escape.

Each person has one.

Be compassionate.

Because your empathy in how others handle their difficult days will boomerang back to you when you're having a down day and need something to escape. In other words, let the person without sin cast the first stone ... and remember, we all tend to sin.

Summertime Blue Skies with Red-Hot Lipstick:

June 18

Ah, summertime is a beautiful thing. After the long cold winter and springtime bloom, all the green leaves are on the trees, life thrives, and love is in the air.

In the winter, it seems as if getting the gumption to get dressed for the cold is difficult. Skirts and bitter wind-chill factors just don't go together. In those days, how you may wish for June. It is the month when the summer solstice arrives and weather is better. It's also a time to put your best foot and best face forward in approaching each day.

So with summer right around the corner, don't be afraid to let your colors emerge just like the flowers of spring. In the heat of these days, do something to make yourself feel special and beautiful...such as a brighter shade of lipstick or a colorful dress.

By doing so, you'll make everyone around you glad that summer has finally arrived!

Let's Go Skinny-Dipping:
June 19

Swimming naked can definitely be one of life's sheer delights.

Whether it be in a pool, a lake, an ocean, or even a hot tub, the experience of diving in without any clothes brings primal blessings to the depths of our souls.

But why?

Maybe it's because our bodies are composed of so much water, and the bare essential of being back in the liquid with which we are made up of reminds our inner core of home.

Singing a few "alleluias" while we're skinny-dipping can be a profoundly moving, spiritual experience. Try it sometime!

In Love with the Minor Miracles:

June 20

So often we hear how our plans aren't always the plans of our Creator. So many times, in hindsight, this adage is proven true to us. With the perspective of time's passage, we see how obstacles were put in our path to set us on the most perfect course of events.

Those sorts of subtle, minor miracles are truly the forte of God's evident handiwork.

And while those delicate details of coincidence can seem so trivial to us at times, they are often the most important thing in setting us upon our destined paths.

A detour can actually be a blessing if we allow ourselves the open mind to see it as so.

The Learning Curve of Life's Lessons:
June 21

There's a learning curve in *anything* you want to perfect. As a baby, we're born with a clean slate, and as lessons are learned and practice is put in, we become much better.

Think about brilliant musicians or artists. Vincent Van Gogh's early work wasn't as prolific as his later masterpieces. Mozart wasn't a prodigy until after *lots* of practice.

It's like that with anything we try. It takes time to gain mastery.

Our initial efforts aren't as good as those we achieve with practice and maturity.

Teaching your children to learn "how to learn" can bring them a lifetime of joy…not only for themselves, but also for you as you watch them grow because of your fine example.

Hoping to Shine a Crazy Diamond:

June 22

The rock band Pink Floyd came out with an epic song called "Shine on You Crazy Diamond." It is comprised of two separate songs that make up ten musical movements. It is truly a long, yet grand, recording off the "Wish You Were Here" release.

In essence, it's an ode to the original singer who formed their initial direction.

He was to the rest a "crazy diamond," someone who went in a weird path but was still a diamond down to the core. His presence created one of the more epic music groups.

Do you know people you would consider to be crazy diamonds (or maybe loony rubies)?

If so, shine them every now and then when they need some attention.

Their hidden brilliance may astound and surprise you.

The wisdom they possess should be cherished.

Seeking More than the Same Old Song and Dance:

June 23

An old man in Venice Beach, California, once sang a song to me as I was painting a boardwalk mural. He said my artistic endeavor brought it to mind. It went like this:

> "Go on and do whatcha do like ya do 'til ya like
> it ... step back and say 'Good.'
> Go on and do whatcha do like ya do 'til you like
> it ... step back and say '*Good!*'
> Cuz when ya do just what you know you should,
> you give the gift of truly *giving!*"

After singing it to me, he told me how he created it. He was watching his lady friend paint. Then after a while of making progress, she stepped back, examined her work intently for many moments, and finally said one simple word: "Good."

Do you feel that way when you scrutinize what you create? Also, do you feel that way when you look at your children? After all, they are amongst the finest creations you will ever make!

The Merits of Faith:

June 24

I'm sure you feel the same when I say that we've all experienced moments of doubt, hurt, and pain. Unfortunately, some of life's lessons aren't always easy.

Yet, this is where the merits of faith mean the most.

Because if you don't have a firm foundation to stand upon, you can get weathered by the storms life sends your way. That's where it pays to have faith in God and to teach your children that same strong sense of faith in the love the Lord provides.

Faith that things will get better helps us all make the most of even dreary days. And the merits of such faith are that if we keep our wits about us when all seems to be going wrong, things will turn out okay in the end for one and all.

Teaching your kids this kind of faith will serve them well all their lives.

In the Mood for a Soulful Love Song:
June 25

Do you have a case of the blues? If you do, a love song sung to you or that you sing yourself can cure all ills. Love songs have a tendency of doing that.

You may let your voice follow along or just sing silently, but the main thing is that your spirit emits the right notes that resonate inside yourself and others.

So many shut this part of their soul aside, yet there's always a call to let it soar.

When that one song hits you just right, it's as if all is perfect with the world. And when that happens, all troubles will soon drift away.

We all have so many worries that cause us concern; however, the right song at the right time can last for ages … with memories only music can unlock with perfect recall.

Rebel at Heart:

June 26

My dog, Rebel, was one who definitely lived up to his name. There was nothing you could force him to do. On the other hand, you *could* encourage him to see it your way.

When given a little bit of freedom, he always went about doing his own thing, but he also knew exactly where home and love were; therefore, he'd always return much happier.

Most people are like that too. They want a little bit of free rein to roam. And since home is where the heart is, if they know deep down where to find love and acceptance, they come back soon with a rejuvenated sense of strength and stamina.

Unconditional love is a magnet that attracts us all back to the original source; therefore, never be afraid to love unconditionally. Make it a part of your giving heart.

Let Me Be Your Muse:

June 27

For the single mom to be a muse for someone with a talent, she must stride the extra mile in order to inspire. And if the creativity is true, you may be blessed with unexpected gifts.

They may decide to give you the art your presence helped them create. Or maybe their gratitude will be expressed in the wonderful ways they treat you afterward.

When a woman inspires a man, a friend, or her kids, they gain a spark in their heart that can cause them to move metaphorical mountains. Their mind becomes filled with a fire that consumes their artistic drive to forge new ground and create something truly monumental.

Be that inspiration; they won't disappoint.

Something to Strive For:

June 28

When you meet the right person, he seems to give you something for which to strive. The right person possesses an intangible presence that drives us to stay alive...on the inside.

When things have been down too long, seeing this "right" person rekindles hope.

He helps the future to look bright once again in the midst of darkness.

His existence can become shared moments that turn into a lifetime with each other's company, always invigorating. People need people, but the right one provides a ray of light that helps us to continue striving onward. Let him know how much you care.

Life's a Dance that You Learn as You Go: June 29

If today was the last day of your life, what do you think you would do?

First of all, stand up tall and make the most of all that is good that surrounds you. Remember also that two hearts beating together are better than one that beats alone.

If your best friend knew now that his or her days were numbered, would you stay stuck in the same old routine, or would you savor each second with zest and verve?

In the dance of life, there are times for twirls and pirouettes; and yet, at the end of the dance, there comes a time to bow gracefully and give thanks for the chance to dance.

Thus, try to always make sure that your soul is prepared for anything and everything; if you were to die today, would your soul be able to rest in peace? If not, try to live out your life so you answer all those questions existing deep in your heart.

Finding My Last First Kiss:
June 30

As today begins, ask yourself how you can make it one of the best days of your life.

One way to do this is to take yourself out of your ordinary routine in order to allow the miracles of chance to occur naturally.

Another way is to make a call to someone you've been avoiding but meaning to talk to. Or perhaps you can drop in on an old friend and rekindle the good memories you share.

If you meet a new person you're attracted to, take the risk to make that first kiss occur.

You never know, venturing forth out of your comfort zone may lead to your last first kiss. And if that kiss catches the two of you in a state of bliss, the possibilities are endless!

July

Can You Ever Have Too Many Friends?
July 1

A friend in need is a friend indeed.

A person who possesses compassion for those struggling through the game of life can be the exact remedy a weary soul needs to smile. And that smile can last all day and all week if your compassion proves to be the first they've seen in ages. Give it freely.

The friendship you show others in being willing to go that extra mile for someone in need may pay dividends when you happen to be the one who needs a favor.

Good friends are earned over time by caring for one another ... even if your friend happens to be having a bad day. And the more friendships you take the time to forge, the more people you have surrounding you who will always be looking out for your best interests when things aren't going right. Friends are a two-way street. Walk it well!

Reach for the Stars:

July 2

Are you in a state of stagnating cycles? Or are you reaching for the stars?

Life is about always being on the move and perpetually improving.

In a grander sense, though, even the stars are constantly on the move. Some are moving toward our solar system, and others are moving away from us. And it's just like that with all the people we encounter because as we age, people come and go.

Likewise, envision how you would like your life to unfold in the future... and even into eternity. Our actions today *do* have an effect later down the line; therefore, it always pays to keep improving. Tomorrow eventually *does* arrive. Plan for it.

Simply Complex:

July 3

Simplicity is an elegant act of balance, as sometimes saying a little says a lot.

Yet it is often complex for the receiver to comprehend. A simple one-word answer can say it all, and that response can be interpreted in many ways. Often, that's where receiving answers in person becomes necessary. Body language does reveal all.

The look in people's eyes and the timing of a response can say so much too.

A grand example of timing is when a clap of thunder or a flash of lightning right after a profound statement or action can make it seem as though God is responding via Mother Nature.

Stay in tune with those grand coincidences. They can send a timely cosmic signal.

Ringing the Bells of Liberty and Independence:

July 4

The Fourth of July is a special day in the United States of America because it's the day we celebrate our independence. It's a national holiday marked with picnics during the day and fireworks at night.

As a single mother, make sure your kids know the importance this day holds for the liberty and freedom our forefathers worked so hard to obtain for all of us. Because many of our descendents gave up their lives for the freedom we often take for granted, and this is also the case for the troops in our armed services who serve to protect our way of life. They often put their lives on the line so our festivities can be worry-free.

Within the fifty states that make up America, we have the freedom to witness its beauty firsthand without needing a passport when traveling from one state to another. And in crossing the country, we can cultivate wisdom for all the cultures that the world has to offer since so many seek to come and live here from all over the planet.

Thus, maybe your family should take a trip today so that they can expand their frontiers with the peace of mind in knowing that others help assure our safety.

Where There's a Will, There's a Way:
July 5

Perhaps the greatest talent a single mother provides is her overarching love for her children, for her pets, and for her home. After the father is gone, she must make the most of the situation and environment she dwells within. And while it is often frustrating, she holds her head held high and perseveres.

Yet, there's still something missing.

How she longs for the love of a real man who appreciates *all* she brings to the table. Her decisions of youth demand that this man accepts her entire package.

But as long as she's willing to put herself out there to find that knight who rides in on his white stallion, there's a way he can and will arrive to revive her aching heart.

So don't give up on finding love in your life; because where there's a will, there's always a way that it can and will arrive.

Someone Worth Remembering:

July 6

Are you someone who blends in with the scenery, or do you stand out?

I think we all know someone who tries to rise above and be unique. And while those people can rub us the wrong way from time to time, sometimes you don't know how much you appreciate them until they're gone. Then we mourn tremendously.

As a single mother, try to impress upon your children the importance of making a positive difference in this world of ours. Often, the only people we remember are those who did things differently. We may think of them as crazy, yet when they're gone, how we wish we could spend just one more day in their presence.

Life's Too Short:

July 7

When your life is jam packed, sometimes it seems as though life flies by. That's when we often wish there were more hours in each day. However, once all the structure that supports your days is removed, providing unlimited freedom, sometimes it feels as if the time crawls and life is too long.

The essence of life is to find the correct balance between doing and being.

As your life approaches your golden years, make sure that what exists in your soul is passed on to those you love. That's when your creativity and ingenuity mean the most so that your impact can last for generations.

In Search of the Missing Link:

July 8

In the cosmic scheme of things, the missing link appears once we close all the switches in our lives for the karmic electricity to flow.

Sometimes all the coincidences in our lives make it seem as if all the infinite tumblers are falling into place for a lock to open and for a new chapter to begin.

For the single mom, this missing link may come in the form of a wonderful man. Still, try to remember that your children's hidden talents and company are the true keys to opening the lock on your beating heart. Nurture their unique attributes because they possess so much. Their joy in discovering them will definitely bring future smiles!

It Is What It Is:

July 9

On the planet Earth, we live under a sky composed of many colors. Sometimes it's blue; at other times, it's rainy and gray. At sunrise or sunset, it can be a brilliant red.

However, how many times have you looked up into the sky and exclaimed: "My, the sky looks so *big* today!"?

The sky is what it is. It provides the air you breathe and the colors that can affect how your mood proceeds for the day. But one thing we all shouldn't do is take it for granted by polluting it with greenhouse gases or clear-cutting our forests.

The atmosphere you may often take for granted is the air your children will need to breathe in all their years to come. Thus, teach them about Earth's eco-system and how we all play a valuable part in making sure it's healthy for our future descendants.

You never know, your lesson now may be what helps your child save the planet sometime in the future!

Live Life to Never Say "What If?"
July 10

As I've grown older, I've begun to appreciate seeing things through to closure and completion. That way there are no regrets. Once the moment to act is gone, will we be able to face ourselves and *know* that we did the very best with what we were given?

Make the most of each second so you never view your hindsight, asking, "What if?" In other words, there's a peace of mind that exists when you never have to ask yourself, "What if I did this?" or "What if I did that differently?"

So try to live your life so that there aren't any nagging unanswered questions at the end of your life. Also, teach your kids to live their lives this way as well … with no regrets. Help them to do their best at *all* times. And if they don't do it right the first time, enable them to learn from their mistakes to do better next time.

That's the kind of lesson your children will love you for as they grow older.

Patience is a Virtue:

July 11

Sometimes we wish that tomorrow would arrive just a little bit sooner, yet when that happens, often we're forgetting something we should be doing right now. The longing for the next day clouds over our consciousness with what we should be doing at the present time.

Each moment can contain so much.

Do we let it pass passively?

Or do we fill it to the brim?

Is our destiny being fulfilled?

Strive to realize the virtue of patience in your life. Sometimes we have to allow life to come to us rather than trying a little too hard. Our plans may not be God's plans after all!

Patience and persistence pay off in the grand scheme of things; remember that.

Worth the Climb:

July 12

If you've climbed a mountain and taken time to admire the view, it's hard to be simply satisfied with mere molehills.

Each life demands an uphill climb if we live it with God's intentions being honored.

How many of us will endure to enjoy our ninetieth birthday party, where a room full of people all shout out at once, "We love you!"?

The climb from youth to our golden years is a constant struggle. We're not always at our best. Bad days do arise.

Yet if you keep hope in your heart, once you climb your own life's mountain, the view will simply blow your mind and make you smile with unmatched inner satisfaction.

Tougher than I Thought:

July 13

Courage is two things: the conviction of a strong confidence in yourself and an inherent faith in the power of good people. They are diligent concerns for any single mom.

She has so many worries that often rain down gently at first, and then a crack of thunder issues forth the downpour.

In such storms you must be careful to believe in and act on the right things that guide us.

It's tougher than any of us think.

When the sky gushes forth with fierce weather, where do you find soulful shelter?

Courage and faith are essential to ride out these storms. Never give them up.

Let Go and Let God:

July 14

For the single mother, so much of your life revolves around your children. And while it is often so full of young ones, a little grown-up company helps remove discouragements.

Yes, the walls *can* close in a little if we socially isolate ourselves all the time.

When that happens, it's a frustrating feeling.

Any single mom has experienced it too.

When it happens, let go and let God.

A little adult socialization is always needed, and this is especially the case for single parents. Find a way to refill yourself with others so inner refreshment is achieved.

Yet always remember another sort of nourishment, the one that comes from God, from the one who created us. If you need someone to listen, he is *always* there.

Songbird:

July 15

Every bird has its song, and it sings not only to communicate but also because it can.

If you have a young child under five or six years old, buy some day-old bread and take your young one to a lake with geese and ducks. Show your child the joy of how to feed the birds.

When we're young, the inherent happiness of feeding hungry wildlife for the first time may start a habit that brings a lifetime's worth of rewards that you'll be glad you initiated.

One loaf of inexpensive bread can feed so many hungry birds, ducks, and geese.

Doing that with your children may start a trend of charity they never grow tired of practicing.

Always a Bridesmaid, Never a Bride:
July 16

A bridesmaid always takes a close look at the best man in the wedding. He was the one the groom chose to be by his side at one of the most important moments of his life. His best man is a trusted ally and confidant.

If you've attended many weddings as a bridesmaid, you've seen many best men.

What separates them from the rest of the guys at the event?

Once an answer materializes in your mind, search for those qualities in the man you'd want to live with for the rest of your life.

Similarly, what separates the wheat from the chaff?

Your answers to these questions will help guide you in your own search for a soul mate.

Standing on the Threshold:

July 17

If your day is in the doldrums, think about a new plan for the future.

Being at the crossroads holds many possibilities. It is a cusp of life filled with choices. One is to turn back and live life the same way as always. Another is to move sideways as if postponement will make your troubles disappear. The best is to walk across that threshold with the best intentions and chart the uncharted territory.

In that moment, refreshment will arrive in the form of "the new."

A new start with a new part to play on the stage of life requires getting to know the new role. And while it may take time to feel comfortable again, you can be rest assured that its fresh perspective will make you feel young again at heart.

Let's Go Fly a Kite Together: July 18

In our childhood, often a parent will find a kite to fly with his or her young one. And to be honest, I'm not quite sure whose joy is greater when it flies high in the sky. Is it the child or the parent watching the child's amazement? Either way, it's a bonding activity.

And as your children age, many such events will draw parents and kids closer together. Those cherished times may be what memories are made of later on.

What's more, it's often important for you as a single mother to play games with your children and also to let them win more than lose. Teaching them the joy of a minor victory helps them build the confidence necessary to tackle tougher tasks later in life.

Showing them how to succeed enables them to endure life's marathons and trials, with their heads held high.

Buzzing around, Looking for My Honey: July 19

When we look at an ordinary flower, it can seem small and insignificant; yet for the bee buzzing around and looking for nourishing honey, it is an immense treasure trove.

Think about how big that small flower seems to the tiny bee. To it the flower appears enormous. A similar concept is to look at the earth from ground level and then to see it from above while looking out the window of a soaring airplane. Very different indeed!

I call this concept "perspectives of scale."

The scale at which we observe something is different depending on our physical perspective. Just as the buzzing bee seems tiny to us, think of how we seem to God.

Thus, even as us humans consider ourselves to be made in the image of God, maybe there are others in alternate dimensions that see us as small. So teach your kids to have compassion for all God's creatures because how we treat others is how we'll be treated in the grand scheme of things.

Surfer Girl in Search of Waves:

July 20

There are many ways to ride the waves. One way is with a typical surfboard. Another is the smaller boogie board. Or you can just bodysurf.

Regardless, the euphoria of being in sync with a cresting wave provides a joy only truly understood by successful surfing in the ocean ... one way or another.

However, imagine the metaphorical waves we ride while doing our daily activities. Imagine doing a spinning round kick without ever leaving the ground. Imagine soaring through space by seeing the gleam in an astronaut's eyes as they relate their adventure.

Nature is made up of many kinds of different waves.

It pays to ride them all with grace, ease, and flair.

It All Starts with Hello:

July 21

One of my friends from India said hello to *so* many people that he named his Ann Arbor, Michigan, pizza parlor: "Hello Faz Pizza."

Faz passed away years ago, yet he taught me to smile, greet, and accept *all* people we encounter with warmth and kindness no matter how rich or poor, no matter what walk of life, and no matter what culture, background, or religion.

He simply loved *everyone!*

And when he passed away, the sheer magnitude of people who came to pay their respects made this simple pizza man's passing rival a president's funeral procession.

Teach your children to love all they encounter.

In the end, they *will* love you back!

And if you're ever in Ann Arbor, Michigan, stop by his restaurant and cherish all his photos on the walls that his wife still leaves up for all to remember him and smile.

The Pursuit of Happiness:

July 22

Happiness is an elusive commodity, especially for the single mother.

Often you have so many roles to play and fulfill that you don't have time for rest.

If you're facing such a dilemma, try to take special care to set aside one day a week to spoil yourself just a little bit; because when you make the time to fulfill your soul's needs, people will notice the glide in your stride as you balance all your activities.

In these days of constant multitasking, a few moments spent spoiling yourself can make you happy while within even the most tedious tasks.

Never forget to take care of *you!*

You Never Know What Can Happen:
July 23

I'm often amazed at how sophisticated we've become in our technological society. As my dad would say, "It boggles the mind."

Yet for all these electronic devices of convenience that surround us, we should still remember that the soul that exists inside us is not much different from those of centuries ago. It's just that we've adapted our minds to be able to build upon all of our past academic achievements. In other words, we stand on the shoulders of giants.

But what if something were to cause all that technological sophistication to collapse?

Would we be able to go back to self-reliance without the convenience of electricity?

Something to think about…

Life is Full of New Beginnings:

July 24

As a fledgling writer, I had to learn to empathize with my characters well enough that I could hear their dialogue within the context of the stories I had created for them.

In a sense, it is akin to hearing the inner voice of conscience speak within my mind; only that voice had to play the role of the many different characters.

The interesting thing is that as time went on, that voice of conscience soon learned to speak in the tones of voices of my friends and loved ones who had passed away. This was most important the day my dog, Rebel, died. Hours after he was put to sleep, as I held him in my arms he started speaking to my mind for the very first time!

What did he say?

"You can't believe how *beautiful* it is here. I can't wait for you to join me once your work on earth is done and complete, for then our friendship will be eternal!"

Regret Nothing:
July 25

Living a life where you have no regrets is tougher than it seems; and yet, with altruistic conscious choices, it *is* quite possible to regret nothing. It takes time and practice to achieve, though, and daily practice eventually makes it easier.

As a single mother, it may be even a harder endeavor, for perhaps you regret meeting the father of your children with whom a separation or divorce occurred.

But even though that man is absent now, without his presence in your life, you wouldn't have God's supreme gifts bestowed upon you—your children.

Never forget that your kids are a gift from the Lord. And while you may struggle to put food on the table and a roof over your heads, when you receive their hugs, kisses, and joyous smiles, it becomes easier not to regret your actions to bring them into the world.

If There's No Wind, Row:

July 26

When you give your love, you get love back in return.

In the winds of change, often we need some sort of anchor to provide stability if the winds get too strong. Love tends to provide that necessary stabilizing element. And the nice thing about it is that you can raise that anchor when you need to set sail.

Where there's a will, there's a way. So if the lack of changing winds brings a sense of stagnation, don't be afraid to pull out the oars and row.

Necessary changes sometimes require proactive participation.

This enables you to reap the rewards you envision on the shores of your promised land.

Boys Need Not Apply:
July 27

A single mom typically has a few boys running around the house, so when she's looking for a solid relationship, the last thing she wants is another boy disguised as a man.

It's funny how making money at an early age can keep a man stuck in his boyhood because typically, some struggles are necessary to turn that boy into an adult.

And a lonely mother raising her kids needs a grown-up masculine figure in her life.

Therefore, when she puts a "help-wanted" sign on the Internet via her personals profile, she's not willing to settle for someone who doesn't understand the role required.

In other words, aim higher.

Street Smarts Beat Book Smarts:

July 28

When I was a young man, I possessed book smarts in abundance. Then, when I left my corporate career, my *true* education truly began in earnest.

One lesson I had to learn *many* times was that what some people say is "the real deal" is just a scam to try and make some easy money off someone who doesn't know any better.

As the saying goes, "If something sounds too good to be true, it usually is." People just don't give away too much without some sort of price attached. There's always a catch, especially with people you don't know.

As I've learned, "The middle man always gets his cut." In other words, if someone does something for you, they usually expect to get something in return. That's just the way life seems to work.

Always be aware of possible false promises. They thrive in abundance these days.

No Negativity, Please:
July 29

A Chinese proverb says, "Flowers leave their fragrance on the hand that bestows them."

Isn't a pleasing fragrance a delightful thing? It says a lot about the person who brings it to you too. It shows that person cares enough to share some kind of wonderful.

Yet when a foul odor occurs at a person's arrival in your life, always be aware, as stinky smells signal an omen of bad tidings somewhere on the horizon.

Always pay attention to all the signals your senses detect.
Each one is a message for you to decipher.
Ignore them only at your own risk.

The Joy of Being a Positive Person: July 30

Give gifts with the essence of newness.

Try to eat food that still possesses a sense of freshness.

For example, processed fast food doesn't have the same taste as something home cooked with loving care. The difference between the two is perfectly obvious and distinct.

One is quick and easy. The other is a labor of love. And in the long run, the positive feelings you receive from something fresh and alive is vastly better than a quick fix.

The more you fill yourself with quality and the positive aspects of life, the fresher you feel inside to help your soul stay alive for ages and ages to come.

Standing Still in a Whirlwind: July 31

July 31 is a special day for me. It marks the anniversaries of my first communion and the day I left my corporate engineering career behind.

Those two days, twelve years apart, mark moments when my roots with God grew much deeper. And from what scriptures seem to imply, twelve is a holy number. So my decisions on July 31, 1983 and July 31, 1995 seemed to have divine importance to me.

This is important too because when you're standing in a whirlwind, you need to stand upon a solid foundation with strong spiritual roots to keep you from being blown away. For me, my fulcrum decisions on this day, years ago, helped provide that firm footing of faith that I still stand upon to this day.

Gale forces may blow, but with divine stabilization, you can endure almost anything the darker forces of life may bring you. Spiritual attacks do occur. The Lord can help.

I hope your roots are planted in deep and fertile soil.

August

Where to Begin...

August 1

As a writer, I often find the blank page daunting. For lonely single moms, the prospect of how to find someone to love can seem similarly frustrating.

The question of where to begin looms large in any endeavor.

Yet, as a wise man once told me, "Don't do something because you think it'll bring a lot of money or success. Instead, do what you love, and all the rest will come naturally."

Truer words were never spoken.

If people see and experience your zest and joy because you put love into all you do, you'll eventually attract the right people to make your hopes and dreams a reality.

Even Nurses Need a Little TLC:

August 2

I know of a nurse who wants to have her life's story become a movie someday. She describes her vision as a blend of *The Notebook* and *The Bridges of Madison County.*

Powerful romance indeed!

And in listening to her tales, she added that her happy ending didn't occur until after a tailspin due to drug addiction. That's when her first love reappeared, turned her mind away from the next fix, and focused her on more heavenly rewards.

He provided the extra tender loving care she needed to see past the escape of addiction. She's now living out her dreams of living with true love each and every day.

If she saw this and changed, so can you!

Hearing the Music of Life:
August 3

Listening to the piano prelude to Johann Sebastian Bach's "Well-Tempered Clavier," I feel a state of bliss in being able to absorb such sweet sounds. Similarly, playing percussion in my church's gospel group, I often feel a sensation of divine tingles and goose bumps. It feels as if our music reaches God's ears, and he responds with a definite sense of divine warmth.

Filling your soul with such inspirational music is what makes the difference between a smile and a frown, even when all the chips seem to be down all around you.

And while we often need loud, rockin' music to release our pent-up passions, hearing the pleasant and pleasing music of life often makes us feel as if things *will* get better soon.

Even if you have no stereo to listen to, just take a step outside and listen to the birds chirping, the wind blowing, the rain falling, or the acceleration of a passing car. There's always something out there for you to hear if you just tune your ears accordingly.

Sports Fan Seeking Teammate:

August 4

When your kids play sports at an early age, they learn that they can't do it all. Rare are the occasions when you can single-handedly win a game all by yourself.

Life is about teamwork.

This is why you should encourage your children to play sports. The game provides a fun way to learn the fact that if we all work together as a well-oiled machine, we *can* succeed.

Likewise, in relationships, we often need each other's help to achieve the overall goal and reach our destined destination.

When we work together with a trusted teammate, we *do* eventually see that promising light at the end of a long tunnel.

There will always be times when nothing will get done unless you do it yourself; and yet, learning to work together is what helps us all make the biggest strides of all.

In Search of Male Stress Relief:
August 5

Single mothers have it tough. They work *so* hard to make ends meet.

That's where some male stress relief is often needed. And as much as you need that special man, chances are that he needs you too.

It doesn't mean you need a companion of the opposite sex to be happy. But if you do have a mate, try to make sure the two of you balance each other's needs and desires.

The blend between testosterone and estrogen shouldn't tip the scales. They should be like a sine wave that swings between two extremes so their needs eventually get fulfilled.

It's like being on a seesaw. You only get on that tee-ter-totter if your weights approximately equal each other so that your combined actions make it fun.

Love is a Hot Spice:
August 6

Love definitely presents itself in a wide variety. Sometimes it's cool and soothing. Other times it's hot, spicy, and passionate. However, it *is* grand.

Imagine a life without love in it. It would definitely feel empty, don't you think?

Love contains the power to forgive, to let go, and to start over with high hopes.

Also, though, it possesses the power to survive for years and years to come.

So as a single mother, if you find yourself with a little heartburn due to having had your heart broken in the past, please don't abandon its ability to spice up your life in order to put a zesty skip in your step. Love never dies, but it does hurt sometimes.

As the saying goes, "It is better to have loved and lost than to never have loved at all."

Love always finds a way ... allow it to warm your heart with the spice it provides.

What am I Doing Here?

August 7

Sometimes we wonder why we're in the frustrating situation we're in—why, why, why?

Long ago I was asked about my feelings on fate. I responded with this: "Fate is a function of choice."

Our choices make up the direction in which our lives ultimately head. Along the way there are triumphs and defeats, but with seeing things on the grand scale of our soul's eternal destination, they all comprise the fabrics we weave into the tapestry of our soul.

What kind of tapestry are you trying to create for your life?

Is it ornate, intricate, and of high quality?

I truly hope so. If not, change!

Friendship is an Excellent Way to Start:
August 8

When desiring a solid relationship, think about how much time you take to groom your friendship before actually entering into physical intimacy.

Typically, the longer you wait to be intimate, the longer the relationship lasts.

Why is this?

Perhaps because when you build your union on a firm foundation first, the established friendship simply makes all the other aspects mean much more.

Friends first; intimacy after.

Always Be Yourself:
August 9

So many people we encounter wear metaphorical masks that hide their true selves. It seems as if they're afraid to let their real feelings be shown or revealed.

It's really a shame that these people feel the need to filter all they say and do.

Just imagine if we all learned to be ourselves at all times without the game playing.

You see, when you try to be 100 percent truthful, sometimes you tend to scare others. They're so used to all the roles people tend to play that an honest soul disarms them.

Perhaps they prefer all the filtered emotions instead of reality.

Yet, don't you think that God loves for you to be yourself? I do.

Pencil Me In; I'm Subject to Change: August 10

Today's title was something I once overheard a young man tell his girlfriend in our Seattle apartment complex's elevator. Upon hearing it, I laughed and shook his hand.

Change is good, which is why it's often nice to use pencils instead of pens, which make a permanent mark.

My first masterpiece drawing was done exclusively in pencil and eraser. It was a nice way to draw too. And often what I artistically did with the passionate strokes of the eraser was more powerful than what I achieved with the pencil lead alone.

Pencils allow the freedom to change your mind without making a mess. Learn from that.

Look into My Eyes:
August 11

Back in 1999, a Detroit radio station counted down their top five hundred songs, and Peter Gabriel's "In Your Eyes" was number one.

And as powerful as his music in that song is, the message its lyrics and title convey is infinitely more powerful.

Quite simply, the eyes are the windows to each of our souls.

When they look straight at you, there's no doubt that that soul is right with you.

When they're looking away, you know that they have other things on their mind.

The eyes often say more than our words, so it pays to pay attention to their focus.

Tomorrow Will Be Better:

August 12

A wise woman once said, "The reason we should do right today is tomorrow."

Think about that quote for a while.

Let it sink into you all day.

It makes so much sense.

How we prepare for tomorrow is crucial.

Everything we put into our actions today matters later.

We *can* build a vast portfolio that can have impact in the years to come.

Anticipation of the next step helps us best know what it actually takes to get there in the present moment. Each second adds to a sum of the ones before. They evolve into a lifetime of actions bundled together that determine if we ultimately achieve our goal. If we don't think today what needs to be done for the future, how can a dream succeed?

Can We Be Nocturnal Friends?

August 13

Walking into a store for a cup of coffee, I produced a handful of change to pay and was a penny short. Then, searching, I found an extra nickel. The clerk, a single mom I'd known for a long time, smiled and said, "Don't worry about the penny; I wouldn't want to leave you cents-less."

Ha ha! Those are the nice laughs you share with a nocturnal friend at five o'clock in the morning. Admittedly, those kinds of smiles were produced amid yawns between us both, but the fact remains that that small joke produced mutual smiles nocturnally.

Ah, the beauty of life never ceases!

A nocturnal friend can produce a friendly smile, even when you're both tired.

Tired of the Games People Play:
August 14

As a single mom, I'm sure you can empathize with today's title only too well. You're tired of all the runaround.

Sometimes I bet you just want to stand up and scream, "I'm mad as hell, and I won't take it anymore!"

Yet if life makes you feel this way, don't give up.

We all get fed up with the mind games people play at times.

However, that's where grace and patience come in. They are virtues in an often weary world. Never give in to the shortcomings of others. Stay strong and at peace.

Are You Hot for Teacher?

August 15

As a kid, I had a crush on one of my junior high school teachers.

One time my aunt took me downtown to see a stage play, and the play's program had an ad in it with my teacher's picture. As I recall, I brought it to her attention. She was quite impressed that I had discovered she did some freelance modeling.

Then, when us ninth graders had a dinner dance, even though I went with a date, I remember asking that teacher to dance with me, which she did. And then, being even a little bit bolder, I asked for her to be the one I had my photo taken with.

Yes, I guess we all can be a little hot for a special teacher in our youth. Were you hot for one too?

The Bikini Effect:

August 16

Many times, hidden treasures are more provocative than the bare facts.

"The bikini effect" is a part of humanity that says it is better not to show it all at once. Leave something for the mind to fantasize about, for once all the naked truth is revealed, we're often turned off by what we see. Maybe it isn't as good as we'd imagined after all.

Be careful what you wish for because it is rare that the fantasy lives up to the reality. And even if it does, there's always the chance of disappointment down the line. Sometimes it's better to let the imagination work its magic via "the bikini effect." Pondering all the potential possibilities can be fun too!

In other words, don't be too quick to reveal everything all at once because what's inside a person is more significant than what they look like on the outside.

What's beneath the surface often matters more.

A Recipe for Love:
August 17

Any gourmet chef knows that too much of any one ingredient overpowers the dish. That's where practice and experience pay off. It's where it pays to know how much is too much of any one thing.

Likewise, when you're concocting your own recipe of love, always try to find that fine line that balances everything nicely.

Too much physicality weakens.

Too little communication leaves it lacking.

Your friendship together is that which warms the dish to perfection.

Love's recipe is one that can be passed through the generations; therefore, don't be afraid to communicate its intricacies so your children reap their own recipes of love too.

How Do You Tell a Good Egg?

August 18

When looking at an ordinary egg, it's difficult to know what's inside of its hard shell.

On rare occasions, you might even discover two yolks—twins!

We all have a shell that surrounds us, which you only let a privileged few crack through.

Knowing the difference between a good egg and a bad one takes time and experience to ascertain, and once you discover it, that secret will stay with you the rest of your life.

But it still takes breaking a lot of eggs to figure it out firsthand.

Driving on Desire:

August 19

God doesn't withhold when we do right and keep our head held high … it's just a matter of *when.*

You and I desire so much, but if we haven't earned our rewards, they will be delayed.

Those delays might be meant to save us in some way from a major disaster that would have soured the reward and made things worse. When they occur, continually ask yourself what still needs to be done before the next step can manifest itself.

By driving yourself on a desire to get the small things done *right,* that's when the delay is removed, and your intended time track of cosmic participation unfolds.

Don't forget the small things. They often matter the most.

The Dog Days of Summer:
August 20

Once the end of August arrives, it seems that those hot and scorching days of summer begin to wane, and the cooling relief of autumn starts to appear near. By this time of the month, you might even see a few leaves on the trees changing color.

It can be a welcome change from the heat and humidity that those "dog days of summer" contain ... days when you see dogs panting to keep cool in the summer sun.

When my dog was still around, I'd always be impressed with how much he enjoyed sitting outside in the shade; and as the sun shifted the shadows as it continually crossed the sky, he'd make sure he was always as comfortable as he could be by moving from one shady spot to another. It made me appreciate his intelligence even more.

The lesson you can learn from this is to make sure you protect yourself from the sun's damaging rays when temperatures are extremely hot. Keep yourself hydrated and make sure you and your kids have plenty of sunscreen while you savor the summer sun.

Communication is My Specialty:

August 21

In-depth intellectually stimulating wordplay seems to be becoming one of our lost art forms. With interruptions from television, cell phones, and videogames, it is growing more and more difficult to have an uninterrupted heart-to-heart talk.

This is an especially important activity to participate in with your children on a consistent basis ... because the better communicators they become, the more their maturity and acceptance amongst others will soar.

Sometimes, being disconnected from the world for a while enables your family to become much more connected to God. And isn't better to be eternally bonded with him?

Therefore, if you want a special night, unplug all the distractions so you can all focus on the basics. Our ancestors did; so can you.

Sing a Song Deep in My Heart: August 22

Singing a song to serenade your loved one is a special way to win a place in his heart.

Even better, though, is to go out into the depths of nature and sing for God alone. When you sing for him, and his sentient creations around you, you let him know how happy you are to be alive.

Sometimes I think he wonders if we appreciate being on the planet he created for us. Sometimes all the man-made distractions detour us away from letting him know how much we care. Sometimes he needs a little reassurance of our love for him.

Don't let information overload detour you away from winning an esteemed place in the heart of our Creator. Sing!

To Sleep in a Bed of Roses:
August 23

When we grow old and finally close our eyes for the last time, the bed of roses we will sleep upon is made up of all our true friends.

Each friend is a different rose.

Some unfurl to expose their full beauty.

Others have an aroma so pleasant we nurture their growth.

Each one seems to possess a unique color and inherent shape too.

While we stop and smell the roses, your children are the flowers that will mean the most in old age; therefore, if you want them to blossom, take time to ensure good growth.

Each flower, each rose, must grow through much dirt to bloom.

Savor each one with a smile.

Deep in the Mother Lode:
August 24

Being a mother is tough. Being a single mother is even tougher. So many worries crowd your mind while making sure your kids grow up knowing right from wrong.

Sometimes it feels as if you've gotten yourself in too deep by bearing children.

If you feel that way, then teach your children the importance of abstinence. It's an important lesson to emphasize too because not only does it teach them a sense of self-control, but it also encourages them to focus on themselves enough to know what they are truly looking for in life and in a mate. That takes time. Teaching them to focus on who they want to be before bringing kids into the world will enable them to thrive later on.

Working to Love the World:
August 25

The love you put into this world is the love you get out of it. What you reap, you shall sow. It's the law of karma.

To love the whole world is a difficult task. It requires many leaps of faith. It also involves tolerance and appreciating diversity.

Prudence in whom to trust is a virtue. Yet, with personal interaction, we learn.

It's an education that never stops. Just when we think we know it all, something comes around the corner to surprise us.

Loving the world requires loving yourself first. Once you enjoy your own soul, you can finally achieve peace of mind when within the company of others.

Class, Elegance, Style:
August 26

Every once in a while an epic woman comes around. She has it all—the physical, the emotional, the intellectual, and the spiritual.

She also feels somewhat lonely.

She sees most men as somewhat primal.

How her heart yearns for the man who is her equal.

Even if you seem to have it all, there may still be something missing.

An epic female needs an epic male.

Such a man and woman search for each other.

When they finally unite, it's monumental in depth and scope.

Their song is complex, yet simply elegant.

Conversations between the two earn many eavesdroppers.

Their act of lovemaking shakes the foundations of heaven and earth.

Thus, if you're a single mom with class, elegance, and style, search every avenue for the man who completes you. The two of you just may set an example all can learn from … especially your children.

Winning Tricks in the Card Game of Life: August 27

In playing a hand of cards, winning a "trick" is the term used to describe the minor victory of playing the right card at the right time. The more tricks you win, the better chance you have at obtaining an overall victory for that particular hand.

In the card game of life, it takes playing the right card at the right time, all the time, and the essence of being able to do that consistently takes time, practice, patience, and lots of trial and error.

Don't give up on becoming a good player, because when you do, the elegance you achieve is the basis that earns the reward of one thing: Heaven.

Will You Make My Telephone Ring?
August 28

Isn't it a frustrating thing to be in a relationship and to always be the one to call first? Don't you wish that your mate would initiate more of the telephone contact?

It's a nice feeling to hear the phone ring and to discover it's your loved one. It's even more special when you're not expecting it at all, when he just called to say hello. Better yet is to have him call just to say, "I love you. I miss you."

Proper telephone etiquette in making each other's phone ring is a delicate dance of balance and actively thinking about the one you love.

The more you give, the more you receive.

Life Goes on Even if the Grass Isn't Mowed: August 29

One summer while growing up poor, due to my dad not sending the child-support checks, our grass didn't get mowed at all because our lawnmower broke, and we didn't have the extra money to get it fixed. Needless to say, our acre of property was an eyesore, and I felt somewhat embarrassed by how our yard had grown wild that year.

Then the next year my mother was able to get a job and purchase a new lawnmower. I couldn't believe the elation and relief I felt over finally having a freshly mown lawn.

In looking back, the lesson I learned was that life still goes on even if the grass doesn't get mowed. You will still live and love and learn even as the grass gets taller than you are. Try to remember that there are more important things than simple chores and outside appearances.

Will You Still Love Me Tomorrow?

August 30

When I faced the prospect of having no home to sleep in, a homeless man stepped up and reminded me to put a penny under the cushion of each shoe. He then quipped, "That way you'll never be broke." That was the ray of light I needed to face my future.

Interesting also was the fact that people still loved me after that torturous time of homelessness was through. They loved me as I once was and loved me afterward too.

If you have people like that surrounding you in times of distress, count them as true friends and companions and then make sure to give them unique gifts showing them you care.

Rekindle the Fire in My Heart:

August 31

When I officially became a writer, I let the flames of love grow low as I persistently pursued honing my creative talents. I bypassed many relationships simply because I didn't want to bring kids into the world while I was still struggling to succeed.

Ten years later, a woman walked into my life who rekindled the fires of love that had grown dormant in my heart. To say the least, I showered her with tons of affection.

The interesting thing is during those ten years without romantic love, I grew much closer to God. Then when that woman entered and brought the fire of my love back to life, the Lord rewarded me with a theophany, a vision of heaven. It was infinitely beautiful! In hindsight, I can see that love was the catalyst. Let love be your catalyst to the splendors of heaven too!

September

Drops of Dew after Stormy Seas:

September 1

In life we all have many storms we have to endure. It does get depressing at times. As summer turns to fall, a feeling of melancholy can set in knowing that winter is coming.

Think about a baby just being born into the world. If it's never experienced winter storms, it can be a little bit frightened. But that's where a loving mother's protection provides peace of mind. After a while the baby learns to adapt. Baptism helps too because it provides a clean slate from the state of original sin we're all born with.

Along the lines of baptism, think of the glistening morning dew. Even after long dry spells, that early morning moisture replenishes our plants just as baptism's water brings joy with the pristine renewal it provides.

God knew what he was doing when he created our ecosystem. He knew that four seasons make our souls more textured. His promises help us weather all the storms.

As the saying goes, "Deferred joys purchased through sacrifice are often the sweetest."

Centerfold Body with a Mind to Match: September 2

There's a saying in Hollywood about the process of making a film that goes like this: "Cheap, fast, good ... choose any two!"

I believe that Francis Ford Coppola, director of *The Godfather,* coined that phrase. In essence, it means if you want something done cheap and fast, then it won't be any good. If you want it completed fast and good, it won't come cheap. And if you want it finished cheap and good, it won't be made as fast as you'd like it to get done.

Likewise, after dating for many years, I made up a spin-off of that saying that goes like this: "Physical, emotional, intellectual ... choose any two!"

This means that if you meet a person who is physically attractive and super smart, he or she might be an emotional basket case. If the person is emotionally passionate and an intellectual powerhouse, he or she probably won't have an attractive appearance. Finally, if the person is beautiful and emotionally stable, they may not have developed a mind to match.

In other words, it's hard to find a mate who has it all. Sooner or later something goes.

Therefore, choose wisely. What means a lot now may disappear in time. People change. Even what was once a centerfold body can start to sag and get wrinkles as the years pass by.

Snapshots of My Life:

September 3

Isn't it amazing how old photos can produce smiles, memories, and even a few tears?

Long ago a friend of mine discussed the inherent quality of a fantastic photograph as a *static* one. It is a moment and expression frozen in time.

He then wondered aloud what *dynamic* qualities a person possesses that separate him or her from a simple static snapshot.

My answer to him was one simple word: "Soul."

Soul is an amazing commodity.

It truly has to be a renewable gift from God.

I say this because each personality is unique and different.

Therefore, perhaps you can pull out an old photo album of yours, sit down with your children and explain why those pictures mean so much to you. Because someday, you might pass them along to your kids so they can remember the young girl you once were with full knowledge of why they are special.

If I Knock, Will You Open the Door?

September 4

In these modern times, everyone expects everyone else to call before they come over to visit. Rare is it for a person to open the door without looking through the peephole. And even then, they still might not open the door if you knock.

When I was growing up on dirt roads with rotary telephones, we didn't rely on making phone calls to set up an appointment. We just walked over and knocked on the door ... or we'd just yell from outside their home for our friends to come out and play.

How times have changed!

Coming over unannounced definitely catches people in their natural state without physical or mental preparation. Then they are who they really and truly are, which can sometimes give more unfiltered truth than if they know you're coming. Choose such arrivals wisely.

A Sip of Champagne to Toast the Town: September 5

Do you ever buy a bottle of champagne to mark a special occasion? If so, do you purchase the finest kind? Or do you try to buy the most unique bottle?

Just as we don't judge a tailor by the clothes on their back, don't be too quick to buy a name brand. For often, the finest quality is found in the rare blends.

It's like that with the men you single moms meet too. Someone who looks like a beggar may have a bank account beyond belief. He just may not want to draw unnecessary attention to his riches and so dresses down. Likewise, the most romantic man may not possess the finest wardrobe.

So if you toast the town, try to do so with some- one who truly appreciates the sights. They may be the champagne that produces the finest inebriation ... that of love!

Shopping for Love with Double Coupons: September 6

When I was growing up, my single mother always clipped coupons and used them sensibly, since receiving child-support checks was rare. She saved *tons* of money too!

Then, when I was dating in high school, she'd give me coupons for fast food restaurants, which I'd occasionally use to help my meager dating dollars stretch further.

And while this habit got back to my friends, who made fun of me during those young days, enough for them to nickname me "The Coup," their ridicule soon turned to imitation once we reached college, because then I'd become a pro at saving money, while they were always running short. Then they soon started appreciating my thrifty ways, especially when we all graduated, and they had tons of student loans while I had none.

I hope you can learn from this lesson. Those double-coupon deals can help make the holidays even more special when you have a little extra saved to buy your kids the gifts they're hoping will be under the Christmas tree a few months from now.

Candy is Dandy; Wine is Fine: September 7

A rhyme here, a poem there
For those who trust, for those who care.

A bottle of wine with the one you love
Often gives you wings with the grace of a dove.

A buzz for your mind, inebriation for your soul
A kiss on the lips, one which never takes a toll.

For in giving our love to others, we learn how to
dance
But only if we open our hearts by taking that
one chance.

Because chances come in droves, do we try every
single one?
Some may give us a rush; some we might try for
fun.

But in trying a little bit of everything, we learn
about the world;
And in doing so we learn a lot and become the
rose unfurled.

Somewhere in Time: September 8

Today's title comes from the title of the superbly romantic movie of the same name, *Somewhere in Time*. If you haven't seen it, I strongly encourage you to rent or buy it immediately. Oh, and buy a box of tissues too. You'll need them for all the tears of romance you *will* cry upon watching it for the first time.

It tackles time travel in order to be with your true love. It also sends a sign that love lasts eternally in heaven too.

That movie holds special significance for me with the one woman I felt the strongest amount of romantic love for ... years ago. Diverging career paths tore our relationship apart, but during our last week together, at a remote lakefront cabin, we watched that movie over and over as we held each other tight ... for the last time.

It makes me wonder whether we'll reunite in heaven, somewhere in time.

Are Wildflowers Better than Roses?

September 9

A book by Robert Bly called *Iron John* describes the mythical journey a boy must make to become a king among men. One of the stages he describes is that the young man must present wildflowers to "the golden woman." Essentially, it comes down to wooing an unreachable woman by giving her a *wild* gift rather than an ordinary one. His choice in unique and hard-to-find flowers catches her attention, and she gives him a chance his status wouldn't ordinarily allow.

Therefore, ask yourself which kind of flower you really prefer ... wildflowers found in a field or those that are in a garden?

Once you answer that question, make sure to let your kids know the answer. That way, they'll always understand the kind of woman you are, and they may learn to appreciate why you made the choice you decided upon so they can grow in depth.

Often, a bouquet of wildflowers picked by your child in a field can mean so much more than a rose bought at a store. So try and teach your kids to appreciate nature's wildness and variety because it may help them find unique gifts not found elsewhere.

There Has to Be Something More:

September 10

Desperation is a difficult feeling to endure.

As the homeless understand only too well, "Desperate people do desperate things."

Why? Because they simply need to survive.

Each one of us has a built-in survival mechanism that often causes erratic actions when all seems to be going against us and when backed into a corner. Hunger, depression, and desperation are a strong mix that can cause actions far out of the ordinary.

During days like those, it gets easy just to give up and give in.

It's only far too simple to take the easy road, sacrifice our moral integrity, and sell a small bit of our soul in the process.

Times like that require the faith and hope in God's promise that there *is* something more.

A Social Butterfly Out of the Cocoon: September 11

Life is comprised of many different stages such as metaphorical cocoons, emergences, and flying free in the currents of change.

One immortal rule to remember is that life is always changing, evolving, and growing.

Yet in order to prepare for the ordeals of the future, we often must endure a sense of slow growth inside a cocoon—one that allows a metamorphosis to occur.

It's kind of like looking at a tiny acorn. What seems so small today has the potential to become a sturdy and towering oak tree decades from now. All it needs is just a little bit of care, water, and fertile soil to grow far beyond what it appears to be when we hold that acorn in our hand, bend over, and plant it in the ground.

Kind and Generous:
September 12

There's a saying in Scripture that goes like this: "How you treat the least of my creations is how you also treat me."

The essence of this quote is that God wants us to be kind and generous to *all*.

This point is especially poignant as the weather is starting to turn colder. During the days of autumn and winter, God's little ones find it even harder to survive.

Therefore, if you have wild animals surrounding your home, think about getting into the habit of helping them cope with the cold. Your generosity could become an endearing habit that will make a few new friends for your children to appreciate once winter arrives. Also, kindness definitely puts good karma into the world that can help you later on down the line.

Dry Humor, Wet Lips:

September 13

If you're a dog lover, today's title might better be, "Dry paws, wet nose." Ha-ha!

I say this because dry paws mean your dog isn't tracking dirt and mud all over the carpet. Also, a wet nose tends to show health in your trusty canine—two good signs indeed!

In your mate, dry humor and wet lips are nice.

Dry humor is that which takes time to appreciate all the subtle nuances, kind of like a fine red wine. Also, wet lips are definitely better to kiss than dry and chapped ones.

Wet and dry—each has its time and place that can send your love into outer space!

Singing is Contagious:

September 14

A musician once said, "Before I could talk, I was singing."

What a way to start off your life!

Yet as a single mother, how do you get your young one to sing before they even learn to start talking? Do this by setting the example even before your child is born.

In other words, when your child is still in the womb, sing! When he or she is born and first placed in your arms, sing with joy! When your child is growing up, sing around the home!

Set a shining example for your children from the moment of conception. They will follow.

Eve Looking for Adam:

September 15

Adam and Eve—God's original human creation.

After making Adam, God soon realized how lonely he was and created a female companion. Can you imagine Adam's elation when he discovered God loved him so much that he made a beautiful woman for him to love?

God's compassion for his creations enabled him to provide an overwhelming abundance for the original Adam and the original Eve.

Now, centuries and centuries later, we are all descendants of his initial creation.

So as you look into the eyes of those you love and feel the warmth soaring through your spirit, take a moment and thank the Lord.

He *knew* what he was doing.

Primetime Player ... Got Game?

September 16

There's a big difference between a true player and someone who is a wannabe.

For those serious about any pursuit, they will always encounter the weekend warrior. Those are the types who don't put in the daily time, practice, and perseverance to get good.

How many work hard with hours of dedicated and focused practice each day to achieve primetime-player status? Most don't like to struggle that much. Many just want to play a game. But for the true player, the score is merely a time-keeping device. It's his love of play.

Long ago in a crucial match, I walked up to my opponent and told him I didn't care who won, just that I was so elated we were both playing at the top of our game. For some reason he couldn't fathom that kind of thinking, and my saying that to him actually threw him off his game, enabling me to come back and win the championship.

Winning isn't everything. What matters is that you love playing the game, win or lose.

It's What's on the Inside that Counts:

September 17

Does a toe-tappin' beat getcha dancin' in your seat?

Has a particular groove made ya wanna stand up and bust a move?

Are your rhythm and blues ample enough reason to spread the good news?

If your answer is yes to any of the above questions, then chances are you have something special inside your soul that counts and matters deeply to God and to all.

If that's the case, don't let the lantern of your love for music grow dim. No. Instead, allow it to shine as bright as a beacon that helps guide others to their greatness. Let the light burn bright so that others crack a smile as they walk that extra mile.

Set the lamp inside your heart on a high mantle so others don't stumble and fall in the forest of their frustrations. Allow it to be a lighthouse to help guide others home safe.

The Eyes Don't Lie:

September 18

When you're speaking with people and they avoid eye contact, do you trust them?

As we age, we learn that a firm look in the eye is important, even more important than what is said most of the time. That and a firm handshake will take you far in life.

So if a person can't keep their eyes on you when speaking, always be on the lookout for what that person's eyes are really focused on. Follow their gaze so you know for sure how much truth exists within their words.

The eyes don't lie.

They speak a wealth of truth.

The eyes are the windows to your soul.

Always keep that in mind with all you encounter.

A Commitment to Love and Loyalty:
September 19

When we make a commitment with what we say, we should make every effort to fulfill our promises so that we earn trust from one and all.

If you can't keep your word, people will soon start to drift away.

It's like the boy who cried wolf. He played games with people so much that when the wolf finally *did* arrive and he cried, no one cared to answer his call.

In other words, he burned all his bridges before real trouble eventually arrived.

Trust is a gift we can give freely along with our love and loyalty. However, once people repeatedly tarnish that trust, they soon realize their mistake when you refuse to be there for them, and then they'll know what they had once you're gone.

Laughter Kills All Ills:
September 20

There's something called the placebo effect, which says that when we *believe* a thing is beneficial to us, regardless of if the active ingredient is present, our belief is actually what cures us more than the actual medicine. Mind over matter.

If you walk around with a constant frown, chances are your body will soon follow suit. But when you put the power of positive thinking to work, miracles *can* and *will* happen.

Laughter and an upbeat state of mind can do wonders for your overall health.

So never be afraid to turn a frown around and into a wide smile.

Belief is one of the most powerful medicines in the world!

Looking for Random Humor:
September 21

Random humor is one of life's true blessings. It comes unexpectedly and brightens even a dark and gray day. Being that you never know when it will arrive, try to stay open to that opportunity to laugh out loud.

Who knows, maybe your child will tell such a bad joke that you'll laugh yourself silly to the point of joyous tears.

Or maybe something will strike your funny bone in a weird way that brings delight.

If your laugh is truly genuine, it will become contagious and create joy all around.

That's Amore:

September 22

Interfaith dialogue is one of the greatest loves of all because it sheds our differences and encourages our unity under our single Creator.

And I sincerely believe that when people from all walks of life find peace and learn to love one another, the Lord says, "That's amore!"

If you were in God's shoes (big shoes indeed!), would you want to see your creations fighting, killing, and causing one another strife? I wouldn't.

I'd hope that each creation could find peace and harmony within all different backgrounds and worldly experiences. I'd also pray that they'd all learn to love one another so that every one of them could experience consistent peace of mind.

Teacher Looking for Class:

September 23

Teachers are a rare breed. If you're one, I bow down and graciously namaste.

When first teaching, they tend to be oh so altruistic. They gain an education to share with our youth. When they're older, it's the youth of their students that keeps them young.

Teachers tend not to get paid as much as other professions even though they should.

Not only do they teach, but they also help, listen, and mold young minds.

Hence, teachers know the difference between someone of quality and those of quantity.

Encourage your kids to be the apple of their teachers' eyes. Winning the trust of a teacher can pay dividends ... especially if they become life-long friends.

This Smile Goes on Forever: September 24

Has anyone said to you, "Smile, God loves you."?

I hope they have, because it's true!

He loves *all* that he creates, even when they fail and falter. If anything, that's the time when you truly need him. And if you do, God will produce a smile that truly does go on for miles and miles.

It's like that famous short saying called "Footprints," where the footprints of you and God are in the sand together, side by side, throughout your entire life. Then the writer notices only one set of footprints when times were their toughest, and he questions why the Lord seemingly left him during those dire times. The Lord replies, "My precious, precious child, I love you and would never leave you. During your times of trial and suffering, when you only see one set of footprints, it was then that I carried you."

The Joys of an Elderly Lady:
September 25

As I was writing today's inspiration, my single mother's ninety-year-old friend called and really brightened my day as we lightheartedly flirted with each other.

She consistently proves to me that life doesn't end when we get older because she still appreciates to get all dolled up, play cards with her gal pals, cook fabulous meals, and polka dance with the best of 'em. I often ask her how many hearts she broke.

I say that because on her 90th birthday party, one of her daughters made a collage of many of her pictures from more youthful times, and I couldn't help but notice how beautiful she was as a young lady … attractive enough that I would've asked her out on a date if I was around her age at that time!

However, these days I just appreciate her wit and wisdom and savor every second I get to spend in her presence. Her old-country laughter always brings a bright smile.

So if you feel sad about getting old, take a lesson from ol' Nellie. She proves to me and to all that life is what you make of it; and in counting the huge number of friends she has, we should all learn a lesson from the joy she still spreads around the world.

Against the Wind:

September 26

Being that I was born in Detroit, it was easy to love Bob Seger songs. Not just because he was a native Detroiter, but also due to basic fact that he sings with deep passion.

And as today's title suggests, his song "Against the Wind" is on the forefront of my mind. I love it due to its sound but also because it describes my life perfectly.

Are you someone who is willing to go against the grain to stand out and be unique?

Are you able to face the currents of change and swim upstream for your destiny?

Do you walk into the swirling winds with a brave courage to defy the odds?

If so, go out and listen to some Bob Seger songs. Afterward, you'll sit content with a slight smile as you soulfully sing along.

Music of the Spheres:

September 27

Bruce Springsteen sings a passionate love song called "Secret Garden." In true essence, every single mom should have a copy of this song, for it truly describes her very well. The lyrics seem to echo the sensual empathy any single mother possesses.

Its passionate saxophone solo is something you should play on your stereo while kissing the main man in your life with all your heart. If you do, a memory will be created that both will never forget. And whenever that song is played, you'll remember that kiss with a smile due to the tenderness the song conveys oh so well.

I myself have a special memory of a special single mom who introduced me to that song. Listening to this song now as I write this, I recall our time together with a wide smile of tenderness.

A Woman over 40:

September 28

If you're a single mom who has just or will soon turn the big four-o, you're savvy enough to know what you're looking for in a man and don't want to settle for less than you feel you deserve.

And while a spring fling with a younger man may help you get your groove back, chances are that his youthful immaturity will leave you looking for something more.

As summer turns to fall at this time of year, those energetic spring flings soon fade, and a desire for a more permanent relationship sets in.

I once saw a student, obviously a college senior, wearing a t-shirt with the slogan: "Freshmen ... get 'em while they're still skinny!" Reading that, I had to laugh.

Yet as youth tends to be free of fat and wrinkles, age brings wisdom and knowledge of how to love. So ask yourself, "What kind of relationship am I really looking for?"

Autumn Delights:
September 29

With autumn's equinox just having past, it's the time when the trees are starting to shed their colorful leaves, giving many of us a lot of raking to do.

Yet, this might be the perfect opportunity to encourage your kids to run and jump into the big piles of leaves. Also, bobbing for apples is another seasonal joy to behold.

After doing just what I described years ago with my female neighbor's kids, she purchased a picture of someone doing the same and gave it to me. In looking at it today, I noticed the quote beneath the drawing for the first time. It says: "The merry heart gives good medicine."

Never feel afraid to share the delights of merriment with all you encounter. The youthful silliness you display to others may be the gift they give to you, which can produce a warmth within your heart years later when you truly need it.

If Hope Floats, Why Do I Keep Sinking?
September 30

As a single mom, it's often easy to feel adrift in a large ocean. And although you may have hope, it can occasionally feel as if you're still sinking.

Life can be frustrating at times when all we seem to be doing is just treading water. If this is the case, don't feel embarrassed to let others know you need help. Someone unexpected may hear your call and come to the rescue.

Often it requires alerting others that you *are* in need. If they don't realize that you need their help, chances are that they'll stay in their ordinary routines. But if they hear your cry, many around you will drop all they're doing to make sure you don't sink and drown.

When you have a need to avoid sinking, allow others to provide the lifeboat and climb in.

October

Compassionate and Unique:

October 1

Do you know someone who seems to be a beacon shining in dark days?

Is that person humble, compassionate, and unique during the storms?

Can they bring a wide smile on a gray and dreary day?

If so, take the time to let that someone know you care.

There's a special lady I know at my mom's senior center who is like this. She seems to strive the extra mile to make all our older folks feel important. Accordingly, I wrote her a touching poem to show how much we all appreciate her compassionate presence.

When she read it, she got a tear in her eye and hugged me hard. Apparently it had been a tough day for her, and she needed a sign to let her know we *do* care.

I guess even the best of us occasionally need someone to lift our spirits too.

Be that person today.

Simple Girl Trying to Avoid the Drama: October 2

Simple minds tend to shy away from the subtle nuances, colors, and intricacies of life. They want everything easy and straightforward in a nicely wrapped package.

But is life truly ever like that?

Drama is a simple fact of life.

As the saying goes, "It's always something."

Each moment contains a potential energy to turn kinetic at any given time. The art of being mature allows you to roll with these sudden changes like water off a duck's back.

So if you find it difficult living a quiet and simple life, take a deep breath, roll up your sleeves, and dive in head-first. The waters of life often require total immersion.

It Might Surprise You:

October 3

To my surprise, my single mom bought a book on *feng shui*. Being the totally over-cluttered pack rat that she is, it was a pleasing thrill to realize that she still wants to try and improve.

For those who don't know what *feng shui* is, basically it's a blend of ancient Chinese wisdom combined with practical common sense to help unleash the potential positive energies that lead to a successful and uncluttered life.

Seeing her read it was a big surprise because she tends to appreciate overabundant clutter rather than minimally elegant simplicity. She often goes into debt trying to save money by buying things at a discount, and any open surface causes her to put something on it.

The fact that she's still trying to learn elegance, though, makes me extremely happy.

Perhaps old dogs *can* learn new tricks if given an environment of love and respect.

Never be afraid to surprise the one you love with a desire to make changes!

If You Could Go Around the World, Would You?

October 4

When the Lord called me out of my original engineering career path to become a writer, artist, and musician, never did I expect to have to travel over a million miles across North America to gain the wisdom and perspective he expected and desired.

Sometimes I felt as if I did it while doing a little kicking and screaming along the way; and yet, he still managed to pull me through it with hope still strong in my heart.

In hindsight, I'm glad he provided the vast education I received. It required venturing forth out of my comfort zone to experience most all of life's facets for myself, often having to sleep on concrete along the way. But the adventures I amassed couldn't be gained by staying poolside at four-star hotels either.

If you were given a choice to travel in order to gain vast wisdom, would you be willing to do it if you had to sacrifice your demanded ordinary comforts? Something to ponder...

Need Your Love:

October 5

Today's title is the name of a song by the band Cheap Trick. I still have fond memories of listening to it in the middle of the night while standing on a lifeguard shack overlooking the Pacific Ocean's majesty from a Los Angeles point of view.

It's a long song, the type that doesn't get any radio play.

Yet in listening to it while overlooking the darkened ocean's vast horizon, I can always go back to that memory and recall my love of the sea's grandeur.

Often our love can transcend that of typical relationships. During those days I needed the love that Mother Nature's majesty did provide in ample abundance, thank God!

So if you find yourself needing love, stay alert. You may find it from unexpected sources.

Humor is the Key:
October 6

Laughter is often one of the best medicines of all. A deep belly laugh can help set all your worries aside in tough times.

So if someone says something truly funny, don't hold back your laughter. If anything, give in to it and laugh until you cry. You'll feel better when you do—trust me.

When God created humor, he gave us the key to releasing pent-up emotions deep below the surface of our emotions. Sometimes we truly *need* that.

I once remember my uncle telling a joke so funny that I literally spit the milk I'd been drinking through my nose. His punch line definitely caught me off guard with a mouthful of milk, and a precious memory was created due to the way I *had* to laugh.

When was the last time you laughed that hard?

If you can't remember, let a little laughter flow!

Checkin' out the Scene:

October 7

When's the last time you moved to a new area and had to reorient yourself to the foreign surroundings? It's a time of getting acquainted with the new environment.

The regulars sometimes don't look too kindly to new blood venturing forth into their familiar stomping grounds and shaking things up a bit. They tend not to like change.

If this is the situation you face, you may not be accepted by all, but you can still try. And along the way, you *will* find a few new friends who accept you as you are. Yet, it pays to realize that being the new kid on the block requires humility and lots of good-natured smiles and handshakes as you check out the scene of your new surroundings.

This is when it pays to be a bit reserved at first but still willing to be open and gregarious at a moment's notice. It's a time of learning to adapt and to roll with the changes.

Life's a Ride; Hop On and Go:
October 8

Today was kind of a sad day for me because I had to take two stray kittens to the humane society in hopes that they would get adopted by a loving family. With winter soon arriving, I could see that they didn't have the survival skills or thick coats of fur necessary to endure the freezing temperatures that were on the way.

And on the ride to the animal shelter, they yelped and meowed often, not really sure what was happening. I tried to reassure them as much as possible by petting them as much as I could, which *did* help. They looked out the windows often, a bit scared.

It was definitely a different experience from driving with my old dog in the car. He loved rides and was always eager to hop in and go.

This time I was taking necessary steps to ensure the survival of two loving feline souls.

Life isn't always the ride we expect or hope for, especially if it becomes frightening; however, if we have someone leading us who has our best interests in mind, our future prosperity may depend on their forethought to make sure we arrive at our destination safely.

Easygoing Easy Rider: October 9

The movie *Easy Rider* was a motorcycle movie that came out many decades ago. It kind of had an eerie ending, but it still made motorcycle road trips enviable.

Having learned how to ride a motorcycle in my teen-age years, I came to realize that I felt the ultimate sense of freedom while riding.

In speaking with an astronaut who rode across the country on a motorcycle, the one point he expressed with emphasis was that when you are on a motorcycle, people are much more willing to come up and talk to you. He felt that without the typical barrier a car provides, people feel more comfortable getting into a conversation. A motorcycle kind of says that you're not on business and are more open to chatting a bit to help pass the day with a fresh perspective.

So if you haven't ever ridden on a motorcycle, perhaps you should try one out. And if you see someone getting off a motorcycle, don't be afraid to ask them a question or two. Their experiences may illuminate you to a world you'll soon adventure into.

Are You Up to the Challenge?

October 10

Life is a series of never-ending challenges.

Each obstacle you face, especially as a single mom, helps determine your ultimate outcome, as well as your children's fate.

So often it seems easier just to give up. If you do, where does that leave you? Essentially, it leaves you back at square one.

Shaking off the rust to rise to the challenge requires a strong will. Courage in yourself and your talents is essential when facing the unbeatable foe.

But even if you fail to win, you will have already won just by trying and seeing it through to determine what result that kind of effort ultimately brings.

Challenges arise, and they are often opportunities to show God what you're made of.

When it Happens, it Happens:

October 11

A saying I often echo to others and myself is, "When you're ready to manifest your destiny, it will come to you."

In other words, we each have a destiny awaiting us, and it takes a lot of *active* participation and soul work in life for these rewards to finally realize themselves.

Just as a long journey begins with the first step, if you hope for a grand reward to appear, you must make the proper actions for it to arrive. That really requires a lot of focus.

With a determined sense of focus, you channel and harness your energies so that the overall effort is directed toward the proper target.

What are you doing daily to make your dreams and aspirations eventually materialize?

Social Butterfly Escaping the Net: October 12

Being a social butterfly takes lots of work. It demands fluttering from one event to the next frequently. And while it may feel nice to get out and about all the time, eventually your body and soul require rest and lots of it.

Sometimes being at home all the time feels like being trapped in a net, and all you long for is a sense of escape.

When is enough, enough?

When is too much socialization too much?

When does being away from home become a bad thing?

If you have children who need your parental participation, perhaps you already know, deep down, the answer to the above questions.

Saleswoman Needs a Closer:

October 13

When working in sales, there is a sense of teamwork required, which sometimes seems like a case of good cop/ bad cop. Typically the good cop role is played by the person who interacts with the customer face-to-face. The bad cop role is performed by the manager, who presents the actual overall price, often, again and again.

Whereas a salesperson gets the customers on base, it's the closer who hits the homerun that brings them to sign on the dotted line to complete the sale.

In any sense, teamwork is essential for the deal to be done and for both sides to walk away happy, as win-win relationships are always best in the long run for all.

Like in any good relationship, each person has a role to play. Play your role well!

Where is My Romeo?

October 14

William Shakespeare wrote, "Romeo, Romeo, wherefore art thou, Romeo?"

Ultimately, *Romeo and Juliet* is one of those timeless classics written by a master scribe, one of the true greats whose work stands the test of time.

So in educating your children as a single mother, do you encourage them to turn off the television in order to read such masterpieces? I hope so.

The more often you get them off of video games and into books will provide them with a *much* greater chance to succeed in the future.

Emphasizing education is one of the more crucial roles a parent must play.

The prosperous future of your kids requires it these days.

I Can Only Imagine:

October 15

I think almost everyone has heard John Lennon's classic song called "Imagine."

It ponders living without war, without prejudice, without betrayal, lies, hatred, and so on.

In my opinion, there *is* such a world; and for me, it exists in heaven because there, God only allows the *good* things to thrive, survive, and be alive.

And maybe that's why it pays to practice shedding all your negative feelings now, because if you don't, will you ever reach that utopian paradise God promises?

Endless Trail of Disappointment, Be Gone: October 16

In choosing to remain single for the forty years I've been alive so far, I've faced many moments of loneliness and disappointment; however, it's also enabled me to possess the freedom to make an impact in the lives of the many woman I've met along the way.

In our culture, we have a strong encouragement to get married at a young age, yet do we really know who we are and what we want during those years?

It often takes some aging, experience, and wisdom to ascertain the wheat from the chaff.

If you've only felt an endless trail of disappointment in your love life, take solace. All those frustrating relationships may be the education necessary to know when your soul mate truly does arrive, and then you *will* be ready.

Fresh Air Needed:

October 17

When the air around you gets too clogged with any sort of pollution, you often need to step outside for a breather. And while a smoky room is an obvious example of requiring fresh air, another case is discussing too much politics or religion.

Political and religious opinions can often overwhelm those neutral parties who share your company. In those cases, the opinions expressed can be so slanted to one side or the other that your guests may feel a little uneasy, requiring a break to breathe in fresh air.

Therefore, if your company appears to be growing uneasy, don't be afraid as the host to change the subject in order to allow a sense of fresh air to filter in.

Enjoying Life One Day at a Time: October 18

Sometimes we can be looking forward to tomorrow so much that we forget about or neglect the tasks of today. In other words, it pays to stay alert in the present moment.

When I was in engineering, we often had large tasks to fulfill called milestones. One of my managers gave me a wise piece of advice in the psychology of tackling such a tough task. He said, "Break up that large goal into many smaller ones that are more manageable and achievable in any given day. In other words, it takes many inch-pebbles to make and arrive at a completed milestone."

His advice was solid, and I've used it in all I do, especially creative endeavors.

Instead of feeling daunted by the overwhelming amount of work required to reach the overall goal, tackle the task in smaller, more digestible pieces, which eventually combine to arrive at the overall finished product.

Make My Heart Flutter:
October 19

The *pitter-patter* of a fluttering heart warms even the most world-weary soul.

So if you feel your heart fluttering with feelings of love, allow your heart to sprout the wings of desire that transport you to mystical and magical places in your soul.

When you do, people will take notice too. They'll see you as if walking on air without a care in the world, and your happiness will soon become contagious.

A fluttering heart filled with love enables you to fly away to great places without ever leaving the safety of your lover's arms.

If you feel this way, let others know.

They *will* feel your full joy.

Trust me on that one!

If You Need a Smile, I'll Share Mine: October 20

Sharing and caring are two lessons we learn as kids that never grow old. When you care enough to share, you bring comfort to others. And when you provide that for them, eventually they feel a need to give back so that an upward spiral of smiles is created.

Certain commodities, such as grins, can be shared into infinity. Hugs and kisses are other gestures you can give away freely that create a positive feedback loop of warmth, acceptance, and prosperity. Caring for another enough to share shows how good a friend you truly are. So don't be afraid to pass along that wide smile!

Strong Woman Who Doesn't Play Games: October 21

When it comes to relationships, the act of playing games with the one you love can have two connotations. The obvious one is to sit down together and play games of chance such as cards or Monopoly. The other is to test your mate with how much he loves you.

In my last relationship, the woman I was with liked probing to see how much I loved her and whether I was jealous that other men wanted to date her. Those sorts of actions ended up breaking us apart.

Why?

Because I'm a strong man who wants a strong and secure woman who is confident with the love she receives from me, which I actively try to show in abundance.

Insecurity in a relationship only breeds resentment. Be confident in yourself, and all the rest will flow naturally. Still, don't neglect giving the compliments yourself as well.

To Have a Friend, You Must Be a Friend: October 22

In listening to a spiritual radio program, the show's speaker gave a statement on sin that I'd like to share. He said, "Sin is the failure to live your life excellently."

He also said, "Freedom is the ability to do good always." After saying that, he spoke about how living with such a definition made freedom a burden or a heavy weight because we're often prone to doing wrong.

Yet that discussion on freedom, excellence, and doing morally good acts is the essence of what is required to be a good friend to all.

To have lots of good friends in your life, you must strive to be excellent and good at all times, not just when others are watching. Because when you get right down to it, God *is* always watching. In other words, excellence is a habit you should practice each day. If you do, people will notice, and then they will *want* to be your lifelong friend.

Sassy and Sweet, Flirty and Fun: October 23

Do you like to flirt?

Are you somewhat sassy?

Do you enjoy having tons of fun?

Are you a sweet and generous person?

If so, chances are that you are great on a first date. Those are the times when a little bit of chutzpah goes much further than being a bit more demure.

If you're a single mom going out on a first date, try to be a little more outgoing than usual. He'll appreciate it. And if he does, watch out; sparks may fly!

Sometimes you need to put your best foot forward so that your potential mate knows what you're capable of delivering when he first meets you. Men like a challenge. Provide that for him with a twinkle in your eye and a smile a mile wide!

Cuddly Girl Looking for Cuddly Guy: October 24

When it comes to cuddling, women have a stereotype of desiring it much more than men. Many guys tend to shy away from that degree of intimacy. And even if they do cuddle with you, it may not be for as long as you'd like. Men and women are different that way.

Therefore, if you're a woman looking to be held dearly, be sure to look for a sensitive man rather than a macho man.

Whereas macho men may be able to repair your car and fix things around the house with ease, sensitive men will be the ones to give you gifts, write poetry for you, and appeal to the finer nuances of your emotional and spiritual needs.

Ultimately the choice is yours.

One man is broad on the surface.

The other is deep in matters of the soul.

Care to Share Some Vino?

October 25

A bottle of wine is fine when you have someone special with whom to share it. Then the two of you can discuss its subtle flavors and nuances, preferably amid candlelight.

Wine is one of life's finer pleasures, and as its inebriation sets into the two of you, perhaps a few of your inhibitions will get set aside as well, which can really make the evening take a few interesting turns, if you know what I mean.

It induces a rousing round of conversation as the lights are turned low, which causes a sense of sensory depravation that allows the mind to expand in interesting ways.

Good conversations where you lose track of time seem to be a lost art form these days, due to so many distractions. Yet when they occur, you may have a night to remember.

Sassy and Loving it:
October 26

Some women seem to thrill in letting their sassy side shine. If anything, it creates a sense of challenge for your male counterpart. If he's up to such a challenge, the two of you will surely go far together.

But how much sassiness is too much?

Just like with any good dish at a fine restaurant, balance of *all* the ingredients is essential.

So while you may love being sassy, also learn to temper it so as not to overwhelm.

A little sass *does* go a long way.

I Don't Bite ... But I Do Nibble: October 27

Today's chapter title is quite a conundrum.

Some people take huge single bites.
Others snack with many small nibbles.

And it's like that for many choices of life.
Sometimes we devour due to desperation.
Other times we savor numerous small tastes.
Many times we are too finicky for anything at all.
Frequently, the day may require a strong dose of fasting.

Integrity is the key ingredient to knowing what your body truly needs for the day.

Too much of any one thing can lead to trouble. Aching hunger is often a blessing in disguise. Survival of the goodness in your soul is a crucial key.

Kissing in the Pouring Rain: October 28

A kiss is the ultimate expression of nonsexual love for one another. In many cultures, the kissing of both cheeks shows warmth and gladness of another's arrival.

Still, when the kiss is on the lips and when it lasts, it turns into more.

Coupling it with doing so while getting soaking wet shows a passion with which precious memories are made.

Those kisses in the pouring rain show a care rare in many couples today. As the raindrops drip down your faces, a bond is established that proves you are both willing to weather the obstacles of Mother Nature to show your love for each other. Try it!

Small-Town Girl in the Big City:
October 29

If you're a woman who grew up on dirt roads, venturing forth onto the endless paved streets of the big city can produce a slight sense of culture shock.

Small-town values seem a little quaint when swimming with the sharks among all those towering skyscrapers. Those values can get taken advantage of too.

So if you do make the transition from a rural village to a cosmopolitan metropolis, always have your feelers up and be open and eager to learn the ways of the city's culture.

If anything, your grounded upbringing will be disarming to big city folk who aren't used to someone being her real and true self, and that'll be the ace in your back pocket.

Forever Smiling:

October 30

A close friend of mine who passed away a few years ago was always willing to provide a hearty hello, and he was forever smiling. I like to believe that he went to heaven that way too, with his infinite grin gracing God the way he graced so many people during his life. I'm sure that the Lord loves him now and forever.

Perhaps that's why it was always so easy for him to smile—because by being such a friendly soul, he *knew* what awaited him in the realm of eternity.

And while I hope and pray that he *did* make it to his destination in God's paradise, I can't help but hope that *you* will reach that realm too.

Remember, when you're forever smiling, you bring a tremendous amount of joy to *all* those you encounter ... especially yourself when you smile in the mirror.

Costumes for the Occasion:

October 31

For your kids, Halloween has to rank right up there with Christmas as one of their favorite holidays because it gives them a chance to dress up and get lots of candy.

However, for my single mother, I truly think she loves it more than the children who come to get treats from her. That's because she dresses up, decorates the house, and gets all goofy around the youngsters. It gives her a chance to feel young again while she watches all the expressions of the young ones who arrive.

Halloween offers the opportunity for you to put on a costume and do a little role-playing...no matter how old you are. And even if you, as a single mother, aren't going to a party, you can always bring the party to you by dressing up and making the most of the holiday in all the joy you bring to the children who trick-or-treat at your home.

November

Personality a Must:

November 1

Personality and passion—yes, they are everlasting.

Think about what makes up a superb personality. Who knows, you may even want to make a list of attributes you enjoy and admire in those you meet. Why do this?

So you can actively remember these characteristics in order to encourage them in your children as they grow older. Make your kids aware of their positive existence, and they may incorporate them into their everyday way of being.

Remember, a dazzling personality goes far in life and in the eternity of the soul.

Just Being Myself:
November 2

If a seashell was in the ocean,
would you say the shell belonged to the sea?

If the seashell was washed on the beach,
could you say the shell belonged to the land?

If a man found the seashell and kept it,
would you say the shell belonged to the man?

If the man sold the seashell,
would you say the money belonged to the man?

If the man dated and married a woman with the money,
and if they had a child, could you say that *the child
belonged to the ocean?*

Looking for the Real Deal:
November 3

Does certain inspirational music lift your spirits and let it soar? If so, that music was made to be the real deal. So when you allow your children to listen to certain songs, help guide their choices so that they eventually become the real deal too.

Being someone who is genuine takes inputting the correct inspirations. In other words, if you allow garbage to go into your kids, garbage will eventually come out of them.

Another way to look at it is to imagine your children as exotic sports cars. If you owned such an expensive piece of machinery, you wouldn't fill the gas tank with junk fuel, would you? No. You'd fill it with premium.

Do the same with what you allow your kids to fill their minds and souls.

Wish You Were Here:

November 4

Long ago, a young love of mine who lived far away would end her letters and emails to me with, "How I wish you were here."

When I received those special messages, how I'd long to be in her arms once again. The passion she put into her correspondence made me glad that we were a couple. Her letters always made my heart leap with joy when the mailman delivered them to my mailbox. And when they came, I'd turn down the lights, light a candle or two, and savor each word on the unique stationery she'd write them on.

This encouraged me to send her handwritten letters penned by candlelight. She appreciated the fact that I'd spray some cologne on each one and seal the letter with candle wax in order to let her know the ambience with which it was written. Ah, youth!

In this day and age of email, don't forget that a handwritten letter can mean so much more to your recipient than just typing something and hitting the "send" button.

Someone for Everyone:

November 5

Attending a lecture the other night, I looked around to see many couples sitting together and showing each other tremendous affection. In observing their appearance and the way they dressed, I felt that they were all perfect pairings for each other.

It's nice that God created such variety in his creatures that there truly *does* seem to be someone for everyone.

Being alone is nice at times, and often is necessary to focus on completing an important task; however, when the project is done, one of the nicest feelings in the world is to share that accomplishment.

Without people in our lives to share our accomplishments, they just don't seem to be as important … so don't be one to surround yourself with only yourself. Let others into your life so that all those special pinnacles in life mean a little bit more when they arrive.

I Believe in Love at First Sight:

November 6

Love at first sight stirs a deep desire.

It can happen many times within a lifetime, each one striking a different facet of our love. Those facets are each part of the diamond in each of us, and as we age, it seems that our diamond of love gets rotated so that different surfaces shine forth with passing time.

When a lover shines the light into that part of our heart, that particular facet reflects a piercing love that sparkles for all to see.

Which facet gets struck depends on how our experiences prepare the diamond to be positioned when that particular kind of "love at first sight" arrives.

As wisdom grows, our love's diamond sparkles in a way different from our youth; yet if it is tucked away and covered up, the light of a new first love never gets to shine.

It's All About the Wordplay:

November 7

Words and rhymes can fill our times with wisdom, wit, and savvy, but a little bit of wordplay goes a long way when what we say manages to make someone's day.

For example, in the past two days, I handed a special woman two separate poems that helped turn her frown upside down. And while the poems weren't meant to be romantic, they showed her how much her presence means to us all, her true friends.

Wordplay also shows our intelligence to others and enables them to appreciate our dedication to strive to rise above the ordinary.

So don't be afraid to show your wit, for it may be another's inspiration.

Don't Sweat the Small Stuff:

November 8

When traveling up the coast of California many years ago, I met a homeless man who told me something I still remember: "Matter don't matter."

For that little nugget of wisdom, I bought him a beer, and we shared precious stories over some suds.

As you ponder his saying, keep in mind that life is filled with matters of large and small significance. It's up to you to decide how much of the small stuff to dwell upon.

In the grand scheme of things, you really shouldn't sweat the small stuff, and you should try to remember that most of it *is* small stuff.

Keep things in perspective.

Be sure to see the forest through the trees.

Ready for Anything:
November 9

When my dog, Rebel, was still alive, he'd chase away all the cats from our yard. Once he passed away, the wild cats surrounding my home soon realized that he was gone and became much bolder in their attempts to hunt the birds I fed at my backyard birdfeeders. They prowled my yard with hopes of catching their next meal.

So one day, in an attempt to keep my fine feathered friends alive to fly the skies, I bought a bag of cat food. This definitely kept a lot more of the birdies chirping happily too. Also, some of the wild cats and birds have even learned to trust me enough to let me pet them from time to time. This didn't happen when my dog was still around.

The lesson to learn is that *all* of God's creatures need food and love—even the wild ones. And in turn, they may just return the love and care you provide if you keep yourself ready for anything. They like becoming friends with you if you try!

Can Men and Women Just Be Friends?

November 10

When men and women interact, there's always a hidden potential for the spark of romance to ignite and spread into a passionate wildfire.

That potential for possible physical intimacy is always in the back of our minds as the two sexes work together. And when they interact, occasions where we make bodily contact only accentuate the existing friction.

It's difficult not to evaluate how an encounter with the opposite sex would be as a mate. But isn't that part of the spice of life? Those random encounters make us glad to be healthy and alive. Savor each one, as friends today can turn to lovers tomorrow.

Never Judge a Book by its Cover:
November 11

When we open a new book, there's always that urge to flip to the last pages to see how it ends before we devote serious time to it, and I admit I'm guilty of having done it too.

But just think about if we could do that with our lives. If we were to know how our lives would end, would we still have the courage to proceed?

The cover of a book is only a superficial appearance of all the wisdom within it. Rarely does it capture all the treasures contained within. It's like seeing the tip of the iceberg and assuming that's all the ice there is to it.

People are the same way. Their physical appearance rarely reveals the depth of integrity and intelligence in their mind, spirit, heart, and soul.

I Know He's Out There: November 12

For the single mother in search of love, it often seems abysmal that the right man hasn't walked through her door.

Yet that's one good reason why you should advise your kids not to rush into marriage with blinders on when young. As children age into mature adulthood, they learn to know more about what they're truly looking for.

In our youth, the rush of love is overwhelming, but once the initial romance fades, is there enough in common for a sense of permanence to set in? And what's more, when we're too young to know about the ways of the world, what do we have to communicate with our mate in order to keep them by our side when we still have so much to learn?

Our grandparents never even considered divorce, but today we do. With that being the case, teach your children the wonders of the world so they want to go out and discover them. Then they'll have a wealth of experience to share throughout a lasting relationship, where the prospect of raising their kids alone never becomes an issue.

Choosing the Right Road:
November 13

There's an ancient Turkish proverb that says, "No matter how far down the wrong road you go, turn back."

This was precisely the saying that went through my mind as I once encountered a road that turned from pavement into bumpy and wet mud. At the time, I decided it was prudent to turn around immediately, even though the muddy road was a shortcut. And while that detour added extra minutes to my journey, it enabled me to stop at a shop for a soda pop, where the clerk made me laugh *so* loud I thought I was going to drop!

Yet if I hadn't decided to turn around, I never would have experienced that soothing sort of belly laugh. Instead, I may have been stuck in the mud, endlessly frustrated.

Taking a Chance:

November 14

The book of each of our lives can contain many chapters or just a few. The length of each section varies on choice and circumstance.

As internal crossroads are reached, taking a chance to venture into the unknown is scary. It's often only after the pain of staying on the same path outweighs the fear of facing the unknown that we're able to stop and make a change.

Other times, these changes occur because of a death, a new home, a new best friend, or even the love of your life finally arriving at your front door.

Take a chance to love a little bit more, to pray a little bit more, to help others a little bit more, to grow strong, and to become wise a little more each day.

Just remember that we each possess love. Take a chance to let it manifest in your life.

Greek Goddess in Search of Her Apollo: November 15

In Greek mythology, Apollo was the god of music, poetry, prophecy, and medicine, who was later identified with Helios, a sun god.

Also, he was known for his manly youth and handsome beauty.

So if you're one of those gorgeous Greek girls whom many call a goddess, can you imagine the festive Greek wedding that would occur if Apollo actually wanted to marry you?

The Hollywood movie *My Big Fat Greek Wedding* was one of those rare cases in recent years when the film did everything right and created a brilliant masterpiece of romantic cinematic entertainment. Sometime, be sure to watch it with your lover and the lights turned low. You *will* feel closer to each other if you do, with a few laughs as well. And oh yeah, don't forget to bring the Windex!

Can You Keep Up?

November 16

A go-getter kind of gal sets a high standard with which she measures each and every man who walks into her life.

She's often asking, "Can you keep up?"

While this is a great attitude to possess, is it a standard you can maintain for a lifetime?

When your youthful zest enables you to set the world on fire with the trail of excellence you blaze, as time passes, what will keep your fires stoked to continue at top speed?

As we age, our highest gear tends to get lower and lower, so make sure to pace yourself, because life is often a grueling marathon. You don't want to burn out too fast.

Where are the Gentlemen?

November 17

Gentlemen seem to be a dwindling commodity in these days of cell phones and video games. Personally, I learned my gentlemanly ways from my single mother, who made sure I learned her caring lessons well so that I could impress all people in general.

Do this for your children as well.

Make sure your boys know to hold a door open for *any* lady. Teach them to put the toilet seat down after using the bathroom. Have them remember to help a woman put her coat on. Encourage him to compliment any lady he encounters. Let your son know how important it is to be on time for a date. Teach him to treat any woman like a true lady.

These lessons will serve your sons well as they embark upon their adult years, and in time they'll appreciate the moral manners you instilled in their hearts.

A Hopeless Romantic with a Hopeful Heart: November 18

Hopeless romantics are the ones who long for the fairy tale romance to come true in their lives. They hold on with hope in their hearts that they will be the prince and princess who turn into a king and queen in their own niche of the world.

And while that fairy tale may not come true as you always prayed it would, you still may encounter a different kind of romance that sweeps you off your feet in unexpected ways.

If you were to tell me in my youth that some of my best romantic moments were to come after the age of forty, I'd have called you crazy; but that's what my reality actually was.

Never give up hope that the love of your life will arrive. They may be a little bit late, but with patience, that's a payoff sweeter than honey.

Do You Love Like I Do?

November 19

When you're searching for true love, don't be willing to settle for less than you deserve.

Demand the best!

If your love runs deep, don't dig for it in a shallow soul's soil. Go for the gusto!

We only have one chance to live each moment as if it were our last, because once that moment has passed, it's gone. And if you made mistakes along the way, be sure to learn from them for the future moments that will arise.

Your love is one of the most precious gifts you possess. Provide that love only to those who truly appreciate it as you feel it should be welcomed. If you're settling for less than you deserve, you're only shortchanging yourself in the long run. Regret may set in.

Shoot for the stars when it comes to matters of love.

Do you honestly deserve anything less?

Cold Nights in Front of a Warm Fire: November 20

Fire up the fireplace on those cold winter nights. When you do, allow yourself to become mesmerized by the dynamic fire's flickering flame.

Nights like these are when a real fireplace is infinitely better than a gas one. Having been on dates with both, I can speak from experience in saying that the gas one's flames become tediously predictable. They aren't nearly as romantic as a real fireplace. A wood-burning fire takes a lot more work to keep going, but the rewards are tremendously more satisfying in the true warmth and crackling mood it provides.

Also, a fireplace is a great place to sit around in order to tell your kids tall tales that make their minds wonder about all the things our great world contains.

A Lover of Animals is a Must:

November 21

As I was running errands today after fulfilling my more important tasks first, a bald eagle majestically soared right over me. Seeing such grace in the air seemed like a savory omen and a sort of reward for feeding all the animals on my lake before departing.

It was as if God was letting me know that I was exactly at the right place at the right time for him to send me such a beautifully majestic sight.

Seeing such amazing grace up in the air above me filled my heart and soul with a divine fire, a fire that sent tingles up and down my spine, then and now.

If you love animals as I do, take the time to notice them and bless them. They were put in your path for a reason. In hindsight, do you see what that reason was?

Giving Thanks for All Your Blessings: November 22

The Thanksgiving holiday is right around the corner. With this said, have you already purchased your turkey and all the fixings for you and your kids?

Historically, this has been a traditionally American holiday symbolizing when the pilgrims set aside a day to give thanks for making it to the new land with their health intact and with the new friends they made in the native Indians who helped them survive.

For you as a single mother, the biggest blessings you should give thanks for are your children. So take this day to let them know how much you love them and appreciate their presence in your life, because it's easy to take them for granted from time to time.

This also might be the perfect opportunity to teach them how to cook, since there typically tends to be *so much* that needs to be prepared for the holiday meal. This way, once they grow older, they'll have all your recipes in mind so they can impress their future families with how great and inventive you were in their youth.

Wine and Dine Me: November 23

When you go to a nice restaurant with a man, do you dress to the T? Will you be the woman who turns heads? Will you be the one to please?

A bottle of wine with another is nice. A great dinner with a lover is fine.

If he pays for both with a smile, will you abandon him later down the line?

We all have the option to use others to escape the confines of our soul. But if we try to give back abundantly, we may find a diamond among the coal.

Nice dinners out on the town are indeed a blessed thing. But if you don't give back to the one who gave, will he ever produce the diamond ring?

It's something to think about this Thanksgiving season.

Always remember to give thanks to him within reason.

My Kids Are My World:
November 24

When a man dates a single mom, he has to remember that he won't be her top priority all the time. Yes, you will try and make him feel important, but as you juggle all your immediate items for each day, he has to be a little patient.

A mother's world will *always* revolve around her children to some important extent. So as you grow serious with him, always remind him that your kids come first.

However, that doesn't mean that you don't desire his love. If anything, you need it dearly! Chances are, since you're around your children all the time, you'll need a break from the young ones in order to feel like an adult again. That's where a man can come in like a knight in shining armor. If he listens to your cares and concerns with empathy, show him how much you appreciate it so he'll enjoy doing so as your futures unfold.

Bird Lover Seeks the Same:

November 25

Birds are my world, and I hope they fill your days with delight as well. They are extremely bright and intelligent creatures!

If you care to try to communicate with the birds, they *will* respond and engage in a rousing round of bird-chirp conversation with you. They're very talkative too!

One of my favorite things to do on a dull day is walk into a nearby forest and tune my ears to the wide variety of birdcalls I hear all around me. Then, as each one chirps, I try to repeat the pattern it makes, eventually moving on from parroting their calls to actually creating my own response to what they say. They like it when you do this.

What I've discovered by doing this is that my sense of hearing sharpened and improved over time. Paying attention to bird chirps has made me more aware of my surroundings.

Try it sometime and see for yourself. Over time, your sense of hearing *will* improve!

Shopping Season Has Arrived:
November 26

The day after Thanksgiving officially marks the first day of shopping season for the upcoming holidays such as Hanukkah, Christmas, and Kwanzaa.

With this being the case, are you one who gets all your holiday shopping done and out of the way, or do you wait until the last moment?

Regardless, this season of buying gifts can be a little stressful for us all. Whether it is long lines at the cash register or trying to find that special sale item, the *real* reason for the season often gets drowned out by the constant reminders to shop, shop, shop.

It can also be a bit depressing if you don't have enough money to buy all the gifts you'd like to give.

This is where your own creativity can come in handy. Because by making your own gifts, you may create minor masterpieces that become cherished family heirlooms. An ounce of inventiveness can easily replace a pound of purchases because what you make is done out of a love and kindness that echoes the true spirit of giving.

So if you can't find or afford the latest gadget as a gift, create your own! Because isn't something you can't get at a store more endearing than the latest fad?

Tickle the Ivories with Me:
November 27

Have you ever had a man perform a spontaneous piano sonata for you? If so, I bet it was a memorable moment for the two of you.

In taking an atheist into my church to play piano for her, she was hesitant at first when she walked in, but her feelings changed as I started performing. Then she slipped her arm in mine and rested her head on my shoulder as she listened to the ivories echo in God's house.

Afterward when we were walking out, I asked her to dip her hand in holy water, cross herself, and say a prayer. When she did, we exited ... and she noticed something special.

She then pointed to the sky excitedly, and it had a vibrant rainbow in it!

I think it was the first time in a long time that she actually felt God heard her prayer, and he responded with a miracle that made us both smile and feel divine shivers.

Always know that God is watching and listening, hoping to recover his lost flock.

Romance, Desire, Spontaneity:
November 28

Many times, the key to romance and desire is the spontaneity with which you and your loved one respond to any given stimulus.

Change often requires making quick decisions at a moment's notice.

Are you able to pick up and go in a split second?

It pays to pay attention. Are your surroundings conducive to the romance you desire? If not, don't be afraid to make up new plans as the two of you go.

A woman admires a man who can sense how her mood matches the environment she's in because she wants safety. If your mate doesn't pick up on your small signs of discomfort, it might signal a red flag needs to be raised with him to feel more secure in the future as your relationship grows.

Will You Love My Dogs Too?

November 29

Aside from humans, dogs have to rank among the top of God's best creations. They get so excited whenever you arrive, and their joy is often so contagious it brings smiles all day. Another great thing about them is the way their tails wag when they're happy.

Give them love, and they *will* give you so much unconditional love it is amazing.

If you're a dog person and are looking to date, make sure that your mate will love your dogs too. You'll easily be able to tell by how much he pets your dogs when he arrives. If he doesn't bother to pet them, then he probably isn't for you in the long run.

However, if your dogs love him, that's a sign for you to keep him close in your life. Your dogs have acute senses that let you know things you might miss on first and even second observations. If your dogs let you know that they don't trust the person who arrives at your door, take this as a sign to find out why. Their sense can be your security.

Bubbly Personality Within: November 30

Bubbles—they are magical things.
Soda bubbles produce a pleasing taste.
They also can make our hearts leap and sing.

Each one is an individual, a bubble that may soon pop. And if you see it doing so, will you be there to catch it when it drops?

Effervescence is a wonderful delight. It brings smiles to our faces. It can provide nourishing refreshment after life's long and grueling races.

So savor the moments of bliss. Take in the tolls of love.
Each one comes with a story, one that can illuminate heaven above!

December

The Key to Me is Laughter:

December 1

A key is a device or a code that enables a lock to be opened.

So if your key is finding someone who provides relieving laughter, hold on tight and savor all the smiles when you find them.

In discovering that jokester and allowing laughter to pour from your heart, his contribution will be over-whelmingly positive in providing the sort of stress relief that only loving laughter can provide in abundance. Let it thrive and in a sense, revive!

As the laughter unlocks your guarded heart, you'll find a bond that can last a lifetime and provide so many smiles along the way that you'll both be glad and not mad the jokes were made. Sometimes we have to give someone the chance to try that right key.

Sing Me Love Songs:

December 2

When was the last time you sang your lover a love song?

Was there an agenda behind it, or did you just sing to express loving joy?

A love song reaches deep into the heart of its intended audience, especially when the singer sings it while looking straight into your eyes.

Having done that for a few special women in my past, I still recall every nuance of the way their stare pierced my soul and embedded their love in my heart. Without my passionate singing for them alone, the cherished memory would never exist.

Even Frank Sinatra and Elvis Presley knew the power of a tender ballad, and their greatness will echo throughout the sands of time.

Hand-in-Hand Strolls Needed:

December 3

I'm a man who loves to walk with a woman hand-in-hand regardless of whether anyone else is watching.

In seeing so many couples who tend to avoid body contact while in public, I sometimes feel sorry for their souls that they aren't open enough to show their naked love for each other. The love they hold for each other isn't something they should hide!

There's a recent TV commercial that shows a young couple walking together but separately. Their hasty progress makes them divide in order to pass an older couple strolling hand-in-hand with wide smiles of fond tenderness. Seeing them, the young couple looks at each other, they laugh to themselves, and then they clasp hands with wide smiles.

So even as you grow older, don't be afraid to express your care and love via physical contact. If anything, it may set a fine example for your kids to show love to all.

Can You Be Silly?

December 4

How often do you allow yourself to act goofy and silly? If you do, you can create a lot of smiles at a moment's notice. It may make others a little uneasy, but for your young ones, such a special and silly soul is greatly appreciated.

Kids can be naturally goofy at all times; and yet, how often do adults allow themselves the opportunity to feel young again?

When you find a man who can intentionally be a gracious goofball around your children, a part of your heart yearns for him even more because by touching your kids' funny bone in a silly way, he endears himself to your soul as someone who would make a great father figure. Therefore, allow your silliness to flow forth with goofy glee!

Rolling Down the Windows to Feel the Breeze: December 5

When my dog was still alive, he used to love it when I rolled down the windows so he could feel the breeze. This was especially the case when we'd drive down dirt roads because then his country upbringing would refresh his memories of youth that made him excitedly paw at the window until I rolled it down. His happiness was my delight.

And while I still miss him tremendously these days, I recently drove down one of his favorite scenic dirt roads and stopped at his old stomping grounds to shout out at the top of my lungs how much I truly loved him. Strong tingles ran through my soul afterward.

That day I truly felt as though he heard my continued love for him from up in heaven.

Don't ever be afraid to do that for those you love in the here and now!

Will You Write Me Poems?

December 6

About ten years ago I befriended an old man who gave me the shirt off his back the first time he met me. I was surprised at the gesture, to say the least, yet it was just his way of showing generosity amid the poverty he endured daily. He had a long gray beard with an abundance of frizzy hair and was as eclectic as they come.

Sometimes when we'd be listening to jazz, he'd suggest that we take turns writing alternating lines for poems we'd create spontaneously.

It was an interesting way to build and develop a friendship, and the poems were always unique. He'd go in directions I never would have imagined, and in the process I learned the joy of writing poems, something I now share with the women I cherish as a kind of tribute to a poor old man who was rich in creativity and joy before he died.

So if you're a single mom looking for some kind of creative activity to do to with your children, try writing poetry together ... taking turns writing alternating lines. Not only will it create lasting memories, but it'll also be a bonding activity that enriches you and your kids!

Taking a Raft Down the River of Love: December 7

December 7 is my mother's birthday, perhaps the greatest single mom I know.

I've been fortunate to have been raised by her because she consciously chose to place love over money in order to raise us right. She instilled a belief in my sister and me that we should reach for our dreams and aspirations, that love is the greatest thing of all, and that a firm faith in God is essential for eternal peace of mind.

She definitely helped us sail down the river of life and love with hope in our hearts.

So what are the basic values you, as a single mother, teach your kids? Do you enable them to become the best they can be? Do you put their needs before your own?

Love, honor, and cherish *all* mothers.

They deserve all the respect and appreciation the world can offer.

Let's Run Off and Join the Circus:
December 8

If you were to run off and join the circus, many of your closest friends and relatives would think that you'd gone crazy.

To put that in proper perspective, though, I thought that the following quote from Charles Butkowski would be appropriate: "Some people never go crazy...what truly horrible lives they must lead!"

When I first encountered that quote, it was placed on a Los Angeles billboard, and upon reading it, I stopped and doubled over in roaring laughter. Obviously it struck a chord and provided a much-needed smile and belly laugh, as all my closest friends and relatives thought I'd gone crazy to quit my engineering career to become an artist, writer, and musician. In the long run, though, I've found my life to be much more robust and dynamic than any of theirs, with wisdom, compassion, and humility as a result.

So don't be afraid to go a little crazy in following your dreams because insanity is something that is defined only in relation to the surrounding status quo. But if you change the world for the better in the process, then who are the crazy ones?

Karaoke Queen Seeks Karaoke King:

December 9

Singing songs on karaoke night is a great way to express yourself while practicing putting your best performance foot forward, and it also builds confidence in front of crowds.

If you're a woman who looks forward to singing her heart out those evenings, try to find a man who shares those same desires. That way the two of you can be your best singing supporters. Who knows, someone important may hear your voice and find you to be perfect for a creative opportunity, opening a few doors for you along the way.

If all you do is sing in your shower or car, few will ever hear the passion you put into each performance; however, if you take the risk to sing in public, you may find the perfect mate who is also willing to stand on that same stage with you.

And isn't a duet always better than singing solo time and time again?

A Cook in the Kitchen, a Lover Down the Line:

December 10

Cooking a great dish is all about the love you put into the concoction you create. And there's a huge difference between food cooked with love and typical fast food.

The first satisfies deep down to the core with its unique nuances. The other quenches an immediate need that ultimately may leave your stomach a bit unsettled.

With the days getting colder and the nights getting longer, a great and economical date idea is for you to go grocery shopping in order to cook your mate a dish with your own home cooking. It allows you to monitor all the ingredients while your loved one rinses and chops all the rest for you. In the midst of this dish, let your hands mingle while passing the ingredients to each other.

That simple action alone may lead to a special night for the two of you.

Another idea is to teach your kids how to cook so that someday they can fix you a dish that surprises you with their inventiveness in the ingredients they choose.

Spiritual Soul in Search of Love:

December 11

Are you a deep woman who strives to spread her spiritual life onto others?

If you are, many blessings to you! You go girl! Keep the faith!

Spirituality is a fine quality to share, especially when it transcends any single religion. Whereas religion provides roots for where you feel at home, spirituality is the roof that shelters like a big umbrella for many to stand under in a storm, bypassing all barriers.

If your soul is a spiritual one, chances are you won't be satisfied with a date who discards such deep matters. It is one of the areas you shouldn't compromise for lust.

Also, don't be afraid to share your shining spirit with all you encounter. Just make what you say general enough not to offend anyone along the way. It's easy if you try!

The Leather is Black; the Hair is Long: December 12

Long hair and leather on a beautiful woman can send thrills and chills up a man's spine.

Now, *black* leather and long hair show that a rebel still exists in that lady's loins.

Long hair represents an existing state of wildness. It shows that age hasn't tamed you quite yet. It reveals an attractive appeal while tossing it around with reckless abandon.

Leather is special, but it's got an even greater edge when the leather is black. Then it speaks volumes and certainly makes a definite statement.

So as a single mom, if you need to get out on the town, don't be afraid of letting your hair down with a little black leather on. It just may be what you need to feel young again with a wild side that cures all those dreary winter blahs in your pajamas.

Let's Look for the Fountain of Youth Together:

December 13

Youth is a state of mind.

If you let society mold your thoughts and opinions, you will grow old rapidly, yet if you keep the flame burning in your heart, your thirties and forties may only be the start.

It's never too late to find youthful exuberance with a skip in your step—often, it all starts with a smile. Share that smile with someone else, and you may walk the extra mile.

So step outside of the ordinary. There's a fountain of youth in all of our souls. The two of you may need an adventure of love to find it. If you do, you won't mind all life's tolls.

Start fresh each and every day. The youth you desire all starts in your mind. Discovering it with the one you love beside you? It will bring delights of every single kind!

Quest for the Cup of Love and Life:

December 14

The quest for the greatest cup of love of all is the search for the holy grail.

That's a cup that provides a love that lasts for all eternity.

It represents the love that was shared during the Last Supper. It's a symbol of communion that is still honored and invoked on a daily basis around the world.

If you're going to embark on such a quest, make sure you're searching for an eternal love. That's the kind of effort that will satisfy your soul for ages to come. It is one that will bring you *much* closer to God, a noble purpose in life indeed!

With this said, as a single mother, remind your kids the real reason why the Christmas season is so important. The "Christ" in Christmas is there on purpose.

Seriously Seeking Chemical Combustion:
December 15

Chemical combustion usually occurs when the correct catalyst is added, which sparks a mixture past the point of supersaturation.

Supersaturation is a term used in college chemistry courses to describe when a chemical solution is over saturated and looking for and needing the right additive to help the desired result finally to precipitate and form naturally for a successful chemical reaction.

In the physics and chemistry of love, what is the catalyst that enables you to reach your boiling point? What additive brings about combustion so that your love flows forth with an overwhelming abundance?

Something to ponder as you dream for your lover to arrive...

All-In for the Poker Game of Life:
December 16

If you've ever played no-limit Texas hold 'em poker, you know the power of the all-in. While it can offer a tremendous bluffing opportunity, it's also a move that can provide you with a tremendously bountiful winning hand.

Extending this card-playing metaphor to the game of life we live each day, are you willing to put all your eggs in one basket and make a huge bet for the best?

If you win with such a move, the sky's the limit, but if you lose, are you able to shrug it off and still survive? Losing this way can cause a few sleepless nights for sure.

In games of chance, an all-in maneuver can be fun and exciting.

In the game of life, the stakes are much higher.

Risk it only at only at your own peril.

Is the risk worth the reward?

Addicted to That Rush:

December 17

There's a certain rush to every addiction we possess, and in my opinion, each of us typically takes on *three* daily addictions that help us cope.

Those three primal daily addictions are different for each one of us, and they may change with time. As the saying goes, "Habit is only replaced by habit." Therefore, if you kick a bad habit, try to pick up a better one. Replace something that brings you down with something that lifts you up spiritually.

These addictions come in many forms too: drugs, alcohol, smoking, food, gambling, TV, Internet, talking on the telephone, text messaging, religion, exercise, etc.

Each one helps pass the time on a dreary day.

Try to choose three that are healthy instead of three that take you down.

The overall difference is obvious.

Love Sells; Who's Buying?

December 18

Love is the key cornerstone in becoming a superb human being. It allows compassion to flow freely from your soul to all those you encounter during a typical day. And in sharing that love inside you, you make the world a better place for all God's creations.

A strong sense of belief is another precious commodity to possess along with love. Having a reason to get out of bed each morning often requires believing in something greater than the obvious dimensions of space and time that immediately surround us.

Accordingly, Louisa May Alcott, author of *Little Women,* is quoted as saying, "Far away, there in the sunshine, are my highest aspirations. I may not reach them, but I can look up and see their beauty, believe in them, and try to follow where they lead."

Always believe in yourself, your love, and the aspirations that keep you alive with a drive to strive for the best so you can thrive in future times.

Campfire Delights:

December 19

A roaring campfire in the foliage of forest, sky, and stars deserves some marshmallows and a special companion with whom you can share their splendor.

The sky can seem so grand in such moments outside. If so, keep your eyes open to see that shooting star upon which you two can make a mutual wish.

If you saw one, for what would you wish?

With Christmas being right around the corner, your children are obviously hoping for all their Christmas wishes to come true. Yet, this may be an appropriate time to teach them to choose their wishes wisely. Because often, God doesn't give us everything we ask for, and he does this out of our own best interests. In hindsight, it's sometimes easy to see that what we once wished for may have been a blessing *not* to receive.

Be careful what you wish for; it just may come true.

Maybe all you need is right in front of your eyes.

Will You Light My Heart?

December 20

Sometimes our heart seems like a darkened doorway in search of an adventurous explorer who can help hold up a candle that lights a way to our utopia.

So if your heart feels the flame of a fortunate soul standing nearby, let that person know how much their charisma and charm did to mend a broken heart. Taking that chance to introduce yourself to a foreign friend may bring an abundance of fortuitous new friendships that unlock unknown worlds filled with new experiences.

And if they do, you may be able to forget the past you've been holding onto, let go, and become made again, with a fire in your heart that is the inextinguishable flame of love.

The Finer Things in Life Are Free:
December 21

The lights of this holiday season are unlike any other, and the sights are all fine and free.

The start of winter marks the time when the days stop getting shorter and the nights stop getting longer. The winter solstice marks the time of shifting toward lighter days.

Perhaps the lights of the season will sparkle on the ice and snow to bring about a new perspective. Shopping and holiday travel are in fashion right now too.

The solstice brings about hope for summertime bliss. And as the earth begins its march toward spring, you can start to dance to a different drum.

Allow the longer days to reinvigorate you with reinvention of yourself—body, mind, spirit, and soul. Each is important. As the seasons change, so do you, and change is free!

Quality over Quantity:

December 22

In the search for a bounty of blessings, often the wonder of "the one" that means the most is more preferable to the abundance of the many. Quality over quantity reigns.

So if you were given the choice of selling all you own to earn an eternal paradise for your soul, would you hesitate? If you knew that all your belongings were weighing you down from rising to everlasting life, would you make the exchange?

Remember, there are no U-Hauls to heaven.

You can't take all of your stuff with you.

But a wealthy soul is always welcome.

Make it the most valuable treasure you possess.

God will thank you for it when all is said and done!

Puppy Love:

December 23

Is there truly any better medicine than a puppy licking your face? I seriously doubt it.

Medicine is scientifically sound, but a puppy is soulfully sound. Which one is better?

A puppy only knows one or two things: joy and love. And doesn't it want to give both without abandon or reservation? The world hasn't made it feel otherwise.

The same is true with a new relationship that starts with the spark of love and desire. It contains all the infinite potential of a marriage of souls whose love lasts all eternity. If you ever get a chance to experience this again, nurture it with all your might.

The newness of puppy love is one that grows into a lasting companionship for all time!

Shall We Dance?

December 24

Back in the summer of 1997, a romantic Japanese movie came out called *Shall We Dance?* Many years later, Hollywood remade it their way.

In the Japanese version of the movie, a successful Asian businessman learns to dance with a grace, flair, and passion his wife never imagined he possessed. Initially, his drive to learn to dance was brought about with an infatuation with a dance instructor he saw nightly as his subway train passed by her dance studio. However, with her as his muse, he overcomes his initial clumsiness to learn the delicate delicacies of fine dance.

That's when his children start to notice their father isn't the same. He has a spirit in his soul that was absent prior to his lessons. When they confront him with this, he confesses the source of this new happiness. And in the end, they encourage him now to teach his new passion to their mother so they all can live happily ever after. He does, and they do!

Seeing that subtitled movie back in 1997 in Seattle, it made me cry my eyes out.

When you see someone discover a new passion, it's a moment of tearful joy!

Oceans of Bliss:

December 25—Christmas Day

In the seas of love and life, bliss presents itself in weird ways. Oftentimes the sea is still and tranquil. Other times the waves are so high we have to surf in order to survive.

In any case, the fact remains that life is about learning to apply the metaphors we learn in youth to our everyday activities. That's where the environment we create for ourselves and our children is crucial. Genetics play a large role in how our kids grow, but if the most genetically gifted child is surrounded by a stagnant environment, will all those genetic blessings ever see the light at the end of the tunnel, learn survival, and rise above?

With today being Christmas, the gifts you give will have an impact on the bliss of your recipients, so choose the gifts you give wisely. If you give anything that helps their creativity flourish, you may be astounded by the talent they surprise you with later on.

So try to give gifts that plant the seeds of intellectual and artistic abundance.

Also, please realize that today's *true* importance is because of the birth of a child in Bethlehem over two thousand years ago who planted the seeds of truth, love, and belief. And just as his seeds have multiplied exponentially, so can those you plant in your children!

Live Life to the Fullest:

December 26

A friend of mine became one of the world's greatest percussionists and was given the nickname of "Ocean." Hearing that nickname, I commented that that would probably make me "The Trickle." He laughed and said, "At least you're not 'The Desert'!"

As our friendship grew, he encouraged me to live life to the fullest so that my "trickle" could become a vast sea of wisdom and knowledge.

So many people lead sheltered lives inside walled gardens and never learn the hard, cold realities of life out in the real world. Instead of learning real-time truth in *today's* society, they study past history and expect that what applied then applies now. Not at all.

While we should learn from our past in order to prevent repeating old mistakes, it also pays to roll up our sleeves, get out, and swim in the present currents of life. That way we're able to roll with the changes as they arise due to experience in the here and now. Those are lessons you typically don't learn sitting in front of a computer screen. The real world is out there waiting for you. Go to it instead of waiting for it to come to you. Live life actively rather than passively.

Food Critic in Search of Gourmet Chef:
December 27

All of us like to critique the creations of others; however, how many of us are open to the constructive criticism some will provide? And if we are able to listen to where others see fault, how many actually do something about it and change? Change is good.

The upward spiral is better than going in circles. And it is our ability to receive the advice others offer and truly take it to heart that separates the winners and losers.

In sports, there's something known as muscle memory, where you practice so much that after a while you don't have to think about it anymore because it just flows out of you.

Practice is essential to striving to be the best, but if you're repeating the same mistakes over and over, that's where some healthy, neutral, expert advice comes in handy.

Just as a gourmet chef needs a food critic to hone their dishes to delightful perfection, so do we all need a guiding ghost to save our souls from disastrous deeds if we pay attention.

Always be open to constructive criticism, as it can help avoid future pitfalls. Remember too: the reason angels can fly is because they take themselves lightly.

Mend My Broken Heart:
December 28

The story of Humpty Dumpty taking a great fall and not being able to put all the pieces back together again is a children's story I feel we all have to live through at least once in our lifetimes. It's sad when it happens. It's hard to recover from a fall from grace.

One of the hardest things to do is put all the pieces back together again by yourself. If you do indeed suffer a setback, it can paralyze you with a sense of depression so profound that you can never quite recover very quickly.

This is where we need to surround ourselves with people who act as electric blankets rather than those who act as wet blankets. If you find yourself around people who consistently pull you down, you may sulk and stagnate forever. Instead, stick by those who nourish you with respect and love. They're the ones who provide welcome warmth. If anything, this is when your children can mean the most.

The difference you'll see in yourself will be like night and day!

An Oasis of Life:

December 29

An oasis of newfound friendship in deserted days is like the shining ray of sunshine through the dark clouds up above. It provides a sense of hope.

The tropical oasis amid barren surroundings is a blessing for which we should all actively search. And by *active* I mean for you to take the initiative, as the only thing that can keep a train from coming down the tracks is the conductor at the helm.

Demand a better future. Insist upon it. Strive for it daily.

If it is not coming to you, then perhaps you have to go to it.

Success is a complacent creature. It demands active participation.

When you find it, don't forget to give back to those who helped it arrive.

Run Wild with Me:

December 30

When a wild horse is in need of training and discipline to help make it fit for its surroundings, the process of taming and teaching it is called meeking the horse.

In our youth, there is a rebel who likes to roam and run wild without a leash or tether. However, once that rebel learns a sense of home and shelter from all the harsh elements, it gains a sense of appreciation for what's important. It grows to like the love it learns.

Running wild is nice. We all need to do it. On the other hand, once we know that it isn't all it's cracked up to be, we learn to be meek and humble. And in that meekness, we can achieve much more because our aim is focused and not so wildly scattered.

New Year's Resolution for New Love:
December 31

Ah, we finally reached the end of a long year. So many days of survival to reach the end, turn the page, and start anew. With this day being the one we tend to dress up for to toast the town, what do you resolve to do to make the next year better than before?

As a single mother, perhaps you proclaim a desire to bring a sense of new love in your life. If so, just remember that that love may come in a form you aren't expecting and maybe don't want upon initial inspection. Love comes in *all* shapes and sizes. Remember *all* of God's creatures can provide that sense of love such as a dog, a cat, your child's friends, birds, or even a long lost friend who needs your help. Your care of them may bring a bounty of blessings you never expected upon first impression.

The New Year starts tomorrow, so resolve to make it your best ever.

Make the changes necessary for perpetual growth!

Closing Thoughts

I hope that this book has been beneficial to your soul's growth on a daily basis. It certainly has been a blessing to write, for it helped me to see the world through kinder and gentler eyes. It helped soothe a soul that suffered the loss of the best friend I ever met in all the forty years I've been alive and have walked this earth.

His departure to his heavenly home up above took a lot of wind out of my sails; however, writing this book helped refill them once again. It is my wish that these pages have done the same for you too. We all need a daily dose of encouragement that provides a needed pep talk to keep our heads held high and smiling at the sunshine.

In the course of living life one day at a time, we never know what the present moment will produce or what miracle may be around the corner. But if we keep our wits about us when all seems to be lost, we *can* rise above and become better than we ever were before.

Never give up. God loves you!

—Most sincerely, Brian K. Shell